Complete
Book of
JUMPS

Ed Jacoby, MS
Boise State University

Bob Fraley, BA
Fresno State University

Library of Congress Cataloging-in-Publication Data

Jacoby, Ed.
    Complete book of jumps / Ed Jacoby, Bob Fraley.
        p.   cm.
    Includes bibliographical references and index.
    ISBN 0-87322-673-9 (pbk.)
    1. Jumping.   I. Fraley, Bob, 1937- . II. Title.
    GV1073.J33   1995
    796.43'2--dc20

95-2205
CIP

ISBN: 0-87322-673-9

Developmental Editor: Julia Anderson; **Assistant Editors:** Jacqueline Blakley, Kent Reel, and Myla Smith; **Copyeditor:** Barbara Field; **Proofreader:** Gloria Jenkins; **Indexer:** Joan Griffitts; **Typesetters:** Kathy Boudreau-Fuoss and Ruby Zimmerman; **Text Designer:** Bob Reuther; **Cover Designer:** Jack Davis; **Photographer (cover):** John Kelly; **Illustrator:** Paul To; **Printer:** United Graphics

Human Kinetics books are available at special discounts for bulk purchase. Special editions or book excerpts can also be created to specification. For details, contact the Special Sales Manager at Human Kinetics.

Printed in the United States of America   10 9 8 7 6 5 4

Human Kinetics
Web site: http://www.humankinetics.com/

United States: Human Kinetics, P.O. Box 5076, Champaign, IL 61825-5076
1-800-747-4457
e-mail: humank@hkusa.com

Canada: Human Kinetics, 475 Devonshire Road, Unit 100, Windsor, ON N8Y 2L5
1-800-465-7301 (in Canada only)
e-mail: humank@hkcanada.com

Europe: Human Kinetics, P.O. Box IW14, Leeds LS16 6TR, United Kingdom
(44) 1132 781708
e-mail: humank@hkeurope.com

Australia: Human Kinetics, 57A Price Avenue, Lower Mitcham, South Australia 5062
(088) 277 1555
e-mail: humank@hkaustralia.com

New Zealand: Human Kinetics, P.O. Box 105-231, Auckland 1
(09) 523 3462
e-mail: humank@hknewz.com

Contents

Part II Event-Specific Technique and Training 41

Chapter 4 Long Jump 43

Chapter 5 Triple Jump 67

Chapter 6 High Jump 89

Chapter 7 Pole Vault 111

Foreword

In my development and career as a professional track and field athlete, I've been fortunate to meet many helpful people and learn many useful things. After all, I didn't win a silver medal in Seoul and a bronze medal in Barcelona all by myself!

The world of track and field is full of ideas on technique and training, and I've tried to listen to and read about all of them. But to avoid pitfalls, I've learned how to weed out the good advice from the bad. And I've learned that certain coaches in our sport are very special in that they not only know a lot about track and field techniques and training, but they also know how to communicate that information to you.

The *Complete Book of Jumps* is more than good advice; it's a proven program for success written by two coaches, Ed Jacoby and Bob Fraley, who fall in that category of very special coaches. Whether you're a long jumper, triple jumper, pole vaulter, or a high jumper like me, you'll find the information accurate, easy to apply, and highly beneficial to your training and performance.

I endorse the information in this book because I know firsthand that it works. Ed has been a coach for many of the national and international teams I've competed on, and has touched my life and career in many ways. As a collegiate jumper at the University of Southwestern Louisiana, I competed against one of Ed's jumpers, Troy Kemp. Troy was an excellent jumper, and the thing that stood out about him was that he was so technically sound and confident in what he was doing. Ed's son, Jake, was a tremendous jumper—an NCAA and U.S. champion. But his size and build was entirely different from Troy's. This showed me that what and how Ed taught could apply to athletes of all types. As the United States Olympic Committee's high jump event coordinator, Ed has put on many clinics that have benefited athletes and coaches. In my opinion, Ed is one of the best coaches in the world.

Bob's success in teaching pole vaulters is well documented. He's one of the most respected pole vault coaches anywhere, and is a true student of the event. And like Ed, Bob has a son, Doug, who has proven through his past performance that his dad's coaching is world class.

It's about time these two coaches shared all of their proven technique and training instruction with jumpers and their coaches. I wish the *Complete Book of Jumps* had been available when I was younger. Who knows—it might have helped me turn those bronze and silver medals into gold.

Hollis Conway

Preface

Over the years, books on track and field have been directed at the entire scope of the sport. However, our sport is unique in that it is a group of minisports. Coaches are usually assigned to an event or event group, more specifically: distance events, sprint-hurdles, throws, and jumps. We conceived and developed the *Complete Book of Jumps* to provide more detailed information on the jumping events.

Having served as National USA Track and Field Men's Development Chairman, as chairman of the Men's National High Jump event, as assistant coach at the 1992 Olympic Games, and as the 1993 World Championship head coach, I recognize the need for a comprehensive manual for coaches and athletes at every level. As a high school and finally as a collegiate and national coach, I have watched the jumps evolve into a highly technical aspect of track and field.

Although the United States is blessed with an abundance of sprinters and hurdlers, we have yet to utilize our wealth of athletic abilities in the jumping events. In the former Soviet Union and other European countries, coaches take a unique approach to jumper development. Because of the strength of U.S. sprinters in international competition, these coaches steer their best sprinters and most gifted athletes toward long jumping, triple jumping, and pole vaulting. After years of working with these top athletes, they produce perhaps the best group of jumpers in international competition. In this country, we tend to shy away from the technical events, especially in the all-important high school programs, because our coaches lack information and knowledge about training athletes for these events.

Our purpose in writing this book is to provide a manual ranging from the basics to sophisticated techniques and training methods. It is intended to serve a large scope of readers and provides valuable information in a variety of areas. First, for coaches already trained in the field of sports science or physical education, it is a resource summarizing the scientific studies performed on U.S. athletes by the USA Track and Field Development Committee and the scientists assigned to specific field event groups.

For young, emerging coaches or students, this book is a basis for developing their understanding of theories and their ability to teach jumping techniques as they move into the coaching profession.

For the serious track and field athlete who wants high quality training and technique instruction, the book contains many of the training programs, coaching points, and useful self-evaluation tips that have helped build high school stars and Olympic gold medalists alike.

The book is a compilation of information we have accumulated over a combined 60 years of studying, listening to, and coaching athletes at all levels. We have attempted to take the mystery out of a group of field events and to help track and field coaches understand that these skill events are no more complex than the running events. In this country, it seems we are always blessed with a "few great jumpers." With improved understanding and preparation, we could have much more success in the field events, just as we have in the sprints and hurdles.

This book provides the materials necessary for a full appreciation of the jumping events. Part I takes the reader through the many commonalities of the jumping events. It describes principles of biomechanics and scientific theories of training periodization and strength training. It provides ideas and suggestions for the development of technique, highlighting successful performances by elite athletes. Part II focuses on specific technique and training information for the long, triple, and high jumps and the pole vault. Finally, sample workout schedules are presented for each of the events.

We are excited about sharing our coaching ideas and technical expertise with you and feel certain that the book will improve your ability to coach or perform successfully.

Ed Jacoby

Photo Credits

Part I opening photo courtesy of Claus Andersen (© Claus Andersen).

Chapter 1 opening photo courtesy of the Modesto Bee and Troy Kemp.

Chapter 2 opening photo courtesy of Kohei Hajiri and Tim Bright.

Chapter 3 opening photo courtesy of Chuck Scheer and Boise State University.

Part II opening photo courtesy of Claus Andersen (© Claus Andersen).

Chapter 4 opening photo courtesy of Claus Andersen (© Claus Andersen).

Chapter 5 opening photo courtesy of Claus Andersen (© Claus Andersen).

Chapter 6 opening photo courtesy of Michael Lafferty and Boise State University.

Chapter 7 opening photo courtesy of Gary Kazanjian and Fresno State University (© Gary Kazanjian).

Part I   Common Features of the Jumping Events

"Is coaching an art or a science?" The answer to this frequent question is that successful coaching is a combination of the two. There have been exceptional athletes who have known nothing about the scientific factors of human movement, an area now known as *biomechanics*. We have seen many cases of these human geniuses who, because of a God-given talent, are simply better than their competitors. There have been other outstanding athletes who, unknown to themselves or their coaches, were so mechanically correct in their technique that they were able to achieve high standards without even knowing why.

A few years ago, I had the opportunity to do a high jump clinic with Dick Fosbury, well-known athlete and creator of the Fosbury Flop high jump. During the clinic, he told of his experiences throughout his high jumping career. His entire story centered around the strength training methods he used, his coach-athlete relationships, and his emotions after setting a world record and winning the Olympic gold medal.

Next I took the floor to discuss the scientific studies and the findings of research that have been ongoing in the years since Dick retired from jumping. As I went through my presentation, I realized that nearly all of the mechanical techniques necessary for an effective jump had unknowingly been accomplished by this pioneer. Dick is now an engineer and certainly understands the laws of physics and mechanics much better than I. However, at the end of the clinic, he told me how amazed he was by the influence mechanical principles have on high jumping. He said there had been very little thought about such things during his jumping career.

Track and field coaches must understand early on that there are constants in this field of endeavor. To begin with, the concepts of biomechanics, which are based on the laws of physics, *must* be understood in principle. It is not necessary to explain Newton's Three Laws of Motion, nor is it necessary that your athletes be overly concerned with such specifics, especially if they are young and inexperienced. They are there to improve their ability to perform successfully and to enjoy the process, and it is the coaches' responsibility to help them reach those expectations. However, the mechanical laws are where the foundation must be laid.

In addition to biomechanical science, there are the biological constants that are rooted in physiology. Here, too, the concepts must be understood. They are the foundation for progressive development in strength, speed, and power and the ability to achieve peak performances. As coaches, we must draw upon the physiological information that is available to all of us.

Finally, there are the psychological constants that have been around for years but little used by many of us. If you need guidance in the most effective ways to teach a technical skill, you need look no further than Thorndike's

Laws of Learning coupled with the sound psychological theories of "conditioning" and the "whole, part-whole" method of learning. Here is where the "art" aspect of coaching comes in—applying the scientific principles to teaching athletic skills while at the same time dealing with the complicated structure of individual personality.

Because of their nature, the jumping events are considered skill events. Skill development can only occur at a high level if the coach has a good understanding of mechanical principles.

The jumping events have many features in common. All jumps consist of an approach run, a transition of horizontal velocity into vertical velocity, and a landing. Because of these commonalities, there are many carryovers from one event to another. If the mechanical concepts are understood for one, they can easily be applied to the others.

Part I of this book is the foundation, the science, the constant that must be understood by any responsible coach. Chapter 1 explores the mechanical factors common to the jumps, while chapter 2 zeroes in on the approach run. Finally, chapter 3 lays the groundwork for a successful strength and power development program.

Chapter 1
Mechanical Factors

As a coach becomes involved with the jumping events, he or she soon learns that there are many concepts that do not change from one event to another. Therefore, it is important to identify the mechanical principles that enable a jumper to become more effective. The individual mechanical factors that influence the jumping events can be summarized as follows:

- **The speed of the hips at takeoff**
- **The height of the hips at takeoff**
- **The angle of the hips at takeoff**
- **Balance and rotations that occur during flight**

Of the objectives listed above, the speed of the hips at takeoff or foot release is the most critical.

Speed at Takeoff

The speed at which the hips are moving at foot release will drastically affect the ultimate performance of any jump. An athlete preparing to jump is influenced by two distinct forces when making the transition from the run-up to the takeoff. One of these forces is a horizontal component and the other is a vertical component. These component forces control the speed of ground release and the direction the hips travel after takeoff. The basic objective of a good jump is to slow the horizontal speed as little as possible while producing as much vertical force as possible. The problem is that while producing this large vertical force, the hips have to be lowered in preparation for being directed upward; however, as the hips are lowered, horizontal speed generally deteriorates. In each of the jumping events and for each individual athlete, the conversion of horizontal speed to vertical speed is governed by the strength and magnitude of the vertical force that is necessary for the individual event. Thus, velocity and the ability to lower the hips will differ from athlete to athlete.

In the high jump, for example, speed of the run-up is important, but if the run-up is too fast, the takeoff leg buckles, making it impossible to develop the necessary vertical force to clear the bar. Table 1.1 shows the magnitudes of both the horizontal and vertical forces developed during major competitions in the United States.

Dwight Stones, who has been the model for most U.S. high jumpers, was biomechanically analyzed several times in the USOC/TAC Scientific Services Program (Dapena, Feltner, & Bahomonde, 1986). The results of analyzing his jumps show that he has a horizontal velocity of about 7.2 meters per second and a hip height on the last step of 53% of body height (see STO46 in Figure 1.1). In simple terms, Dwight is approaching the bar rather slowly and is higher than most other American jumpers. His perfor-

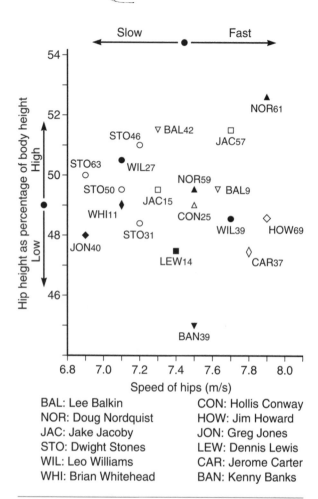

BAL: Lee Balkin
NOR: Doug Nordquist
JAC: Jake Jacoby
STO: Dwight Stones
WIL: Leo Williams
WHI: Brian Whitehead

CON: Hollis Conway
HOW: Jim Howard
JON: Greg Jones
LEW: Dennis Lewis
CAR: Jerome Carter
BAN: Kenny Banks

Figure 1.1 Height and horizontal speed of hips at touchdown of takeoff leg.

Note. Used with permission of Dr. Jesus Dapena and the United States Olympic Committee.

mance for the two major components was *slow and high*, yet he was indeed successful.

Also included in Table 1.1 is the comparative data of velocities and angles of takeoff in the long jump. This data is a composite of many long jumpers' performance over a length of time. Evaluation of this data reinforces the importance of high velocity and low angle of takeoff in the long jump event.

The ultimate high jumper would run in excess of 8 meters per second and have a hip height less than 46% of body height at the beginning of the takeoff. In other words, this ultimate jumper would be *fast and low* going into the takeoff step.

The Russian jumper, Igor Paklin, is estimated to approach the bar at over 8.0 meters per second and his hip height on the last step is 46%

Coach's Tip

Runway speed can only be evaluated at takeoff, no matter what the velocity on the runway. What counts is the speed occurring as the athlete leaves the ground.

Table 1.1
Comparative Data of Velocities and Angles of Takeoff in the Long Jump

Athlete	Horizontal velocity (feet/sec)	Vertical velocity (feet/sec)	Resultant velocity (feet/sec)	Angle (deg)	Distance of jump (feet)
Beamon (USA)				24.0	29-2$^1/_2$
Ter-Ovanesyan (USSR)	28.2	11.5	30.5	22.0	27-5$^1/_2$
Boston (USA)	29.4	10.6	31.3	19.8	27-2
Owens (USA)	27.9	11.6	30.2	22.0	26-8
Robertson (USA)	28.9	10.0	30.6	19.2	26-7$^1/_4$
Schwarz (W. Germany)	31.7	10.6	33.5	18.5	26-2
Shelby (USA)	28.5	10.5	30.4	20.0	26-0$^1/_2$
Baumgartner (W. Germany)	31.6	10.0	33.1	17.5	25-9$^3/_4$
Gloerfeld (W. Germany)	29.4	10.4	31.2	19.5	25-9$^1/_4$
Stekic (Yugo)			30.7	20.0	25-7$^3/_4$
Bell (USA)	27.6	10.8	29.6	21.8	25-5$^3/_4$
Honey (Aust)	25.5	12.7	28.5	26.3	24-8$^1/_4$
Lorraway (Aust)	25.6	13.0	28.7	26.6	24-2
Lewis (USA)	31.3	9.0	31.6	16.5	28-7

Note. Used with permission of Dr. James Hay.

of body height. Cuba's Sotomayor may have a velocity that exceeds 8.5 meters per second with a hip height less than 46% of body height. This incredible combination of speed and body height at takeoff enables him to make a jump of more than 8 feet.

Speed into the takeoff is best generated by using what coaches call the *gradual accelera-*

tion progression. Simply stated, this is a constant increase in both stride frequency and length throughout the entire approach up through the penultimate (next to the last) stride. Any disruption of this constant increase in tempo must be eliminated. The most likely time for speed to slow during an approach is when the athlete begins to settle or lower (transition) in preparation for changing from the horizontal to the vertical. Most problems of slowing are caused by one or all of the following factors:

1. Negative foot speed into the penultimate stride
2. Braking with the takeoff foot (foot too far in advance of hips)
3. Allowing the hips to be too low for effective speed in the running position

Negative foot speed is actually occurring at each foot strike during any running action, but in practice, the athlete wants to keep this retarding action at an absolute minimum.

While running, a certain horizontal speed is achieved by the athlete's hips during the pushoff and airborne (non-foot-support) phases of the stride. As the leading foot prepares to strike the ground, it must be moving backward at the same time the entire body is moving forward. If the foot is moving backward more slowly than the hips are moving forward, or if the foot lands well ahead of the hips at ground contact, the overall speed of the hips is reduced at the instant of foot contact. Thus, it is important that the athlete not overstride and that there is maximum backward foot and leg speed (active landing or pawing action) during foot contact and throughout the support phase (see Figure 1.2).

In a sense, we discussed braking with the takeoff foot while describing the effect of the foot striking in front of the hips. However, this is only part of a potential speed reduction problem. During either the penultimate or the takeoff strides, the foot must be positioned at contact such that it can clear the ground as quickly as possible. During these two critical strides, foot contact is best made by landing flat on the ground. The athlete whose foot lands too

Figure 1.2   Negative foot force occurring at touchdown. Hips are moving forward at 8 m/s. Foot is moving backward, yet forward horizontal foot speed is 1.18 m/s at ground contact.

high on the toes will be forced to settle to a fully flat foot position before ground release can occur. Conversely, landing with the foot too far back on the heel will cause a braking of horizontal speed prior to takeoff.

Finally, getting too low or being out of the efficient running position is common for the inexperienced jumper. An old rule of thumb is: "Low is slow." To run effectively, the hips must be as high as possible. This enhances stride length and effective leg recovery. Although we know this is true, it is also necessary for a jumper to be tall and erect, placing the hips in a position so that vertical force can be achieved at takeoff. The hips should be lowered only by a slight flexing of the ankle, knee, and hip. Thus, the lowering or transition from horizontal to vertical is a subtle hip settling and should not decrease horizontal speed.

Height of Hips at Takeoff

The second factor in achieving maximum hip height is important for all of the jumping events.

As soon as an athlete leaves the ground, because of gravity, he or she begins to fall back to earth. Therefore, the higher the hips due to either body stature or running technique, the greater the potential for a higher or longer jump. A high center of mass means an athlete will remain airborne longer.

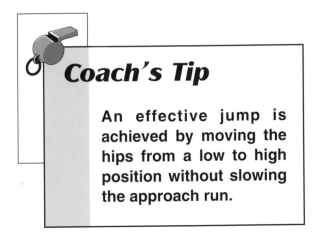

Coach's Tip

An effective jump is achieved by moving the hips from a low to high position without slowing the approach run.

All athletes have a predetermined innate height, a factor that cannot be controlled. However, there are three distinct techniques that aid in raising the center of mass to its maximum. First, the ability to run as tall and erect as possible is essential. During a running approach up through the takeoff, the foot must strike directly under the hips. Any tendency to overstride causes a low hip position.

Second, an effective jumper has the ability to shorten the last stride before moving into the takeoff. Shortening a stride causes the hips to rise. The goal is to allow the penultimate stride to lengthen, causing the hips to lower slightly, then to shorten the last stride, causing the hips to rise to the highest possible position (see Figure 1.3).

The third factor is body velocity at takeoff. This factor has a significant impact on hip height throughout the jump. The higher the velocity at takeoff, the higher the hips will be during the flight curve of the jump. The flight curve of a jump is analogous to that of a projectile shot from a cannon. Picture two cannons side by side and pointed toward the horizon at exactly the same angle (see Figure 1.4). The projectiles in both guns are identical, and the only difference between the guns is the charge of powder placed in the barrels. In one cannon, there is a spoonful of powder, and the other contains a bucketful of powder. The projectile shot from the cannon with the most powder will have a greater velocity than the one shot from the cannon with the small charge of powder. The projectile with the greater velocity will have a much higher trajectory during flight and a far greater range.

Using the same analogy, if a runner moving at 6 meters per second leaves the ground at an angle of 20°, his or her center of mass will rise 7 inches. If the same runner increases velocity to 10 meters per second and leaves the ground at the same 20° angle, his or her hips will rise to 22 inches. Thus, *the faster the athlete's approach, the greater the potential for a better jump.*

Takeoff Angle

The angle through the center of mass (hips) of the jumper is called the *takeoff angle*. The flight path, or parabola, is determined just prior to and during foot release into the jump. Once the athlete is airborne, this directional path cannot be altered. The jumper travels up and down the flight path at the same angle.

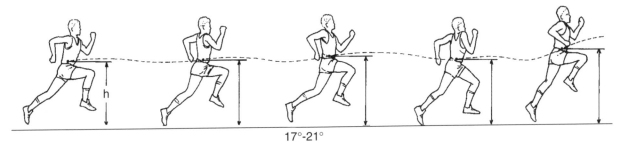

17°-21°

Figure 1.3 Last five steps in the long jump approach, showing rise of hips at takeoff.

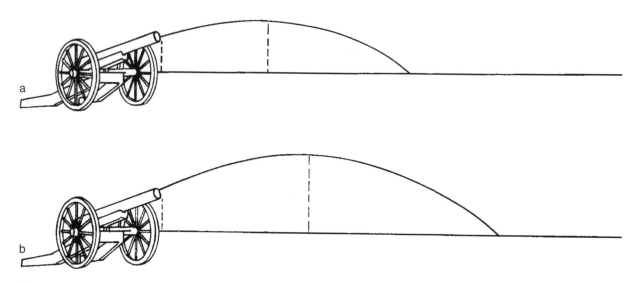

Figure 1.4   (a) Low projectile velocity; (b) high projectile velocity. The projectile with the greatest velocity has a higher trajectory during flight and, therefore, a greater range.

The angle of takeoff is a function of speed. The faster the run-up with no disruption moving into the takeoff, the flatter the takeoff angle. A low takeoff angle is important in the long jump and even more important in the triple jump. The obvious solution is to generate as much speed as possible down the runway and into the takeoff. Maximum speed is important in the pole vault as well; however, the vaulter must also be concerned with creating the highest pole angle possible. The high jump is an exception to the maximum speed principle because the high jumper attempts to create as large a vertical component as leg strength will permit. But even in the high jump, speed is important, and the takeoff angle is much flatter than you would expect. The best jumpers in the world average (and rarely exceed) a 52° takeoff angle. Figures 1.5 to 1.7 show the takeoff angles achieved during the 1987 World Championship meet in the triple and high jumps and the pole vault.

Balance and Rotations

The final mechanical aspect of the jumps has to do with balance and rotations that occur during the flight phase of any jump. The athlete's objective is to move or adjust the parts of the body during flight to take advantage of the already established parabola. The purpose is simply to clear a bar or prepare for an efficient landing.

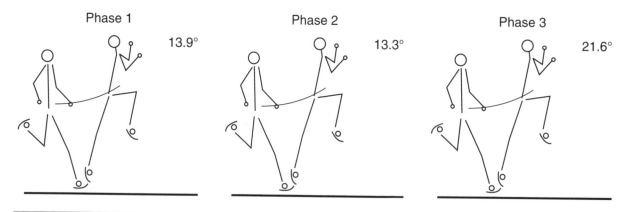

Figure 1.5   Takeoff angle in the triple jump.

Note. Used with permission of the International Amateur Athletic Federation.

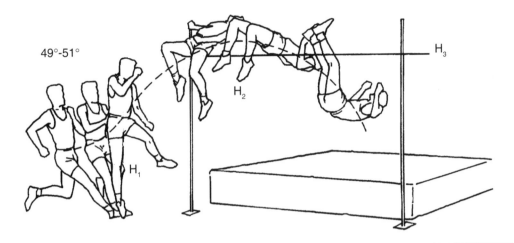

Figure 1.6   Takeoff angle in the high jump.

Note. From "Mechanics of Translation in the Fosbury-Flop," by J. Dapena, 1980, *Medicine and Science in Sports and Exercise*, **12**(1), pp. 37-44. Copyright 1980 by Williams & Wilkins. Reprinted with permission of Williams & Wilkins and Dr. Jesus Dapena.

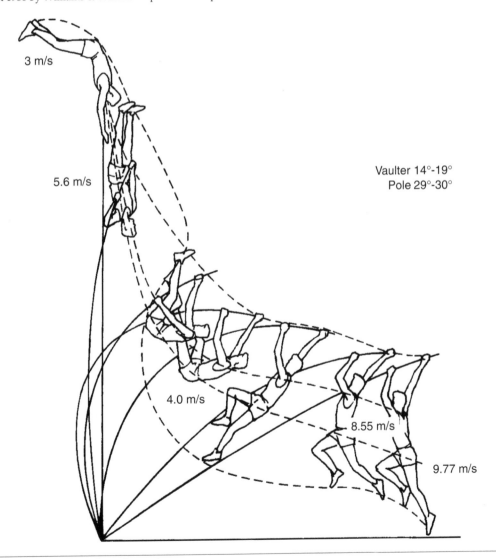

Figure 1.7   Takeoff angle in the pole vault.

Note. Used with permission of the International Amateur Athletic Federation.

Coach's Tip

All jumping events are essentially dictated by the activity on the ground. Direction, power, and forces are established there. Airborne actions generally maintain balance and prepare for a good, safe landing.

As stated earlier, the parabola of the flight path will not change once the athlete is airborne, although the movements of one body part may lift or lower another. This is due to Newton's third law: "For every action there is an equal and opposite reaction." Rotational speed increases or decreases as lever length changes. Lengthening or shortening the arms, legs, or trunk influences the speed or rotation around their axes. The specific rotations vary for each event, but the wise coach will understand their effects on the body while it is airborne.

In the long and triple jumps, the "hinge moment" (deceleration at the foot) causes all parts of the body above the foot to accelerate. Thus, at takeoff there is a tendency for the body to rotate forward. The more efficient the takeoff, the less the rotation; however, some undesired forward rotation will always occur. During the long or triple jumps, the hang or hitch-kick movements can be used to eliminate or delay undesired forward rotation (see Figure 1.8). The hitch kick is a clockwise rotation of the legs that causes a counterrotation of the upper body and thus eliminates much of the rotation developed at takeoff. Regardless of the technique employed, forward rotation in the horizontal jumps tends to cause a premature landing, which is contrary to an effective jump.

Summary

Speed, height, angle, and balance are the four key elements common to all the jumping events. All coaching and technical work must center around these basic mechanical concerns. Speed at takeoff affects flight direction, which is further affected by the angle of takeoff. The height of the hips at takeoff is crucial because gravity pulls on the athlete once he or she is airborne. Finally, balance must be maintained while in flight to capitalize on the athlete's parabola of movement. Any departure from these key elements will adversely affect performance.

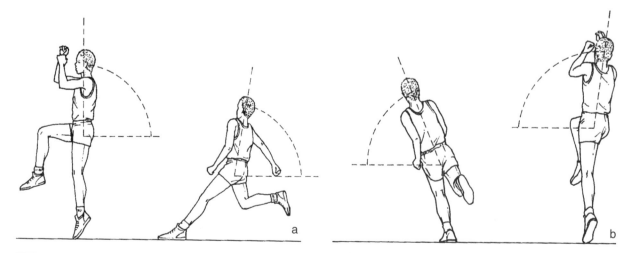

Figure 1.8   Lateral and backward lean at takeoff, as shown from (a) side view and (b) back view. These leans are necessary to establish proper rotations over the bar.

Chapter 2
Approach Run

Although the approach run is described in all of the individual event chapters, you should understand the similarities of all three events and that a single mechanical-technical concept should be used in the long jump, triple jump, and pole vault. The common objective for an approach run in all three events should be to develop as much horizontal velocity as the athlete can handle, converting this horizontal speed into vertical speed at takeoff. The approach run should be thought of as a means of positioning the body in an efficient, upright, and tall body posture over the last four to five strides prior to foot release. You should review the objectives of setting up the proper mechanical situations to ensure an effective jump or vault.

Key principles of the approach run are to

- develop maximum controlled speed at takeoff;
- maintain an upright body posture during takeoff; and
- strive for a low, flat angle at takeoff.

Because these components are necessary to the development of an efficient jump, they should be the sole concerns when developing and working on runway approach techniques.

Acceleration Curve

The desired approach must utilize the "acceleration curve," a concept emphasized by sprinter coaches. The acceleration curve is an athlete attempting to accelerate over a period of time. The distance should follow a set pattern until maximum acceleration is reached. At some point during an all-out effort, the body will reach a peak speed, maintain that speed for a short time, and finally, due to fatigue, begin to decelerate (see Figure 2.1).

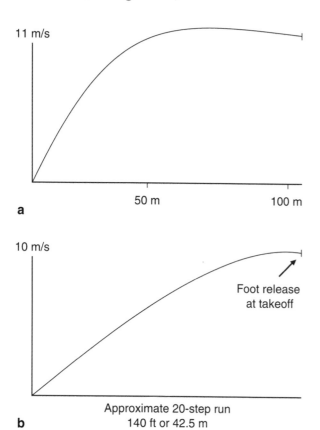

a

b

Figure 2.1 Simulated program of acceleration curve for (a) a sprinter and (b) on an approach run for a jumper.

Each athlete's individual characteristics must determine the length of time and distance to reach maximum acceleration. The takeoff must coincide precisely with this time period. For this to occur, the athlete must understand that each step from the beginning of the approach run until the next to last step gets longer and faster. This is the rhythm or tempo the athlete desires—a constant buildup of speed and frequency

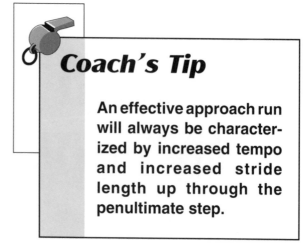

Coach's Tip

An effective approach run will always be characterized by increased tempo and increased stride length up through the penultimate step.

throughout the entire approach. The jumper assumes the same characteristics as a sprinter from the start until 40 to 60 meters into a race.

What is the ideal distance for a jumper to run during the approaches? This is determined by the individual athlete but is controlled by body height, stride length, and the ability to accelerate over time. The principle that must be understood and applied is the faster the athlete, the longer the acceleration process takes. Conversely, the younger or slower the athlete, the less time the acceleration process takes. A young or slower athlete may reach top speed in a few strides, perhaps 20 to 30 meters. A world-class sprinter may take up to 60 meters to reach top speed. Regardless, the coach should work with each athlete to determine this individual difference.

Length of Runway

A general formula for developing runway distances is presented in Table 2.1. Rather than using a measured distance, we use the number of strides throughout the approach. This concept can be used to devise a learning progression for the approach run. As stated earlier, a constant progression of stride length and frequency is important to a successful approach run.

An effective method of achieving this technique is to begin the jumper running from 12 total steps early in the season. To teach the concept of tempo, we instruct the athlete to

Table 2.1
Estimating Runway Distances

Elapsed time (in seconds) for 30 m	Elapsed time (in seconds) for 100 m	Suggested number of strides for approach during competition
4.7	13.0	12
4.5	12.5	14
4.3	12.0	16
4.1	11.5	18
3.9	10.5	20
3.7	10.4	22

stand at a point on the track with the takeoff foot forward. From a static position, the athlete should push out as forcefully as possible and begin counting each time the takeoff foot strikes the ground. The count should go "one and two and three and four," etc., until count 6. At this point, the athlete should pop up in the air to simulate a takeoff. This count system allows the athlete to visualize the increased stride frequency up through the takeoff.

The entire process should take place on the track or grass and always away from the board or vault box. The purpose is for the athlete to become tempo and frequency oriented rather than takeoff board oriented.

As the athlete learns to accelerate and make the transition from horizontal to vertical, the distance can be measured and transferred to the takeoff board, but not until all the required components are adapted by the athlete. As the athlete learns to run from 12 steps, gradually add 2 steps to the approach. Remember, the fewer number of strides, the less chance for mistakes to occur. In our teaching system, all runways from the short approach practice to the major competition run-up are handled with the tempo count system so that it becomes automatic for the athlete. In addition, the coach is better able to determine what problems the athlete is having and when they occur during the run-up.

We always begin the learning process with 6 count steps. In competition, the elite, very fast athlete might require 10 or 11 count steps. The key is never to increase the distance or number of steps when there is any chance of deceleration at the end of the run.

Posture Through the Run

It is important to remember that an inclined body position is a product of acceleration. During the first stages of acceleration, there is a high degree of forward lean. As an athlete reaches top speed, his or her body becomes erect. During deceleration, there is a backward inclination. By simply observing body posture throughout the run, the coach can determine the efficiency of the approach run.

As the jumper's hips move along the runway, they naturally rise to a level position (disregarding the slight undulation due to the running stride). For the athlete to jump, a transition must occur. The center of mass must lower before it can rise (see Figure 2.2). This hip

Figure 2.2   Hip displacement during the last four strides of Carl Lewis.

Note. Used with permission of Dr. James Hay.

displacement must occur in all jumping activities. The athlete must make this transition subtly to maintain horizontal speed; the goal is to lower the center of mass without slowing down. This is accomplished using a somewhat sophisticated technique.

As mentioned earlier, each stride during the run-up should get progressively longer up through the penultimate stride. During the penultimate stride, the athlete begins the transition with a slight increase in stride length (see Figure 2.2). As the stride lengthens, the hips will lower. In addition, through a slight flexion of the knee and ankle joints, the hips will lower even more. This is accomplished by an incomplete extension of the third step before takeoff. This technique allows the penultimate step to be directly under the body with the foot flat on the ground. It is followed by a slight shortening of the last step, which automatically forces the hips into a high takeoff position. The last step should again be flat so a solid, quick impulse occurs prior to foot release. With slight variations, this technique should be used in all jumping events.

Coach's Tip

A forward or backward lean by any running athlete is a sign of either acceleration or deceleration, respectively.

Steering

Although we discussed the technical and mechanical means of achieving an accurate run-up, there seems to be an innate ability associated with an accurate approach. Dr. James Hay, TAC/USOC biomechanist, notes that "for almost 100 years, articles on long and triple jump-

ing have advised athletes they should develop a constant pattern of striding through practice and they should, under no circumstance, look at the board and adjust the length of the strides so they can hit it" (Hay, 1990).

Through a variety of investigations, Hay and others have found that, almost without exception, the skilled athlete looks at the board during the run-up and makes adjustments. This visual control seems to be better in some individuals, but the important consideration is that the "steering" adjustment seems to be complete at or around the fifth step from the takeoff board or vault box. Keep this in mind as we move into the final phase of the runway, setting and using check marks.

Check Marks

Many coaches and athletes dissect and divide runways into a complex and sophisticated means of achieving maximum speed before the jump. They make something difficult out of something that should be simple.

No matter how many steps there are in a runway, a consistent and simple format should be used. The runway should contain three check marks, two of which are not considered specific check marks for the athlete. The most important check mark is the starting point. Our philosophy in teaching a beginning jumper is to use a static start, which is simply a standing or rockback push into the runway. It is a beginning in which the takeoff foot is forward. The athlete pushes hard off the takeoff foot, which is in constant contact with the ground. The body rocks backward, and the athlete simultaneously steps back with the nontakeoff foot and finally pushes out of the backward motion as forcefully as possible.

The static or rockback start allows the athlete to accelerate from the same motion and with the same force each time the run commences.

More advanced jumpers sometimes move into the start with stutter steps and in some instances with bounding strides. We feel this procedure can lead to major problems in the approach.

Of the other two check marks, the first is the actual takeoff board or vault box. The second check mark becomes an important adjustment mark for the coach to aid the athlete on successive run-throughs. This mark is commonly called the "coach's check" and should not be a focal point for the athlete. The mark is placed either four or six steps prior to the takeoff point (see Figure 2.3). Athletes commonly use a specific mark at four steps. Some successful vault coaches use a mark six steps out. This important check mark reveals several things that can make or break a good run-up.

If a long jumper fouls by, say, 8 inches, the remedy is not simply for the athlete to move back 8 inches. If the athlete is looking down at the board in the latter part of the approach, he or she will probably be reaching or lengthening the last stride to hit the board. Moving back causes the athlete to reach for the board even more and almost certainly to foul again.

Recall our discussion about the steering mechanism. The well-trained athlete makes subtle stride adjustments up to the fourth to sixth step out from the takeoff. From that point

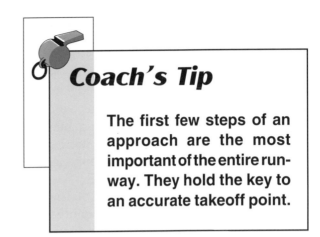

Coach's Tip

The first few steps of an approach are the most important of the entire runway. They hold the key to an accurate takeoff point.

the strides become constant. We want to place a coach's check mark in the vicinity of this natural adjustment. By placing a check mark at the fourth or sixth step, the coach can determine if the athlete should move up or back, and by how much, to achieve an accurate approach.

For example, an athlete starts down the runway and four steps out from takeoff is 8 inches beyond the coach's mark, and the athlete subsequently fouls or has a poor takeoff in the vault. The correct adjustment is simply

Number of total steps

12	14	16	18	20
				R
			L–S.P.	L
			R	R
		L–S.P.	1 L	2 L
		R	R	R
	L–S.P.	1 L	2 L	3 L
	R	R	R	R
L–S.P.	1 L	2 L	3 L	4 L
R	R	R	R	R
1 L	2 L	3 L	4 L	5 L
R	R	R	R	R
2 L	3 L	4 L	5 L	6 L
R	R	R	R	R
3 L	4 L	5 L	6 L	7 L
R	R	R	R	R
4 L–C.C.	5 L–C.C.	6 L–C.C.	7 L–C.C.	8 L–C.C.
R	R	R	R	R
5 L	6 L	7 L	8 L	9 L
R	R	R	R	R
6 L–T.O.	7 L–T.O.	8 L–T.O.	9 L–T.O.	10 L–T.O.

6 Count = 12 Steps
7 Count = 14 Steps
8 Count = 16 Steps
9 Count = 18 Steps
10 Count = 20 Steps

Figure 2.3 Step and count patterns. SP = starting point; CC = coach's check; TO = takeoff. The coach's check is shown at four steps from the takeoff, but could be moved to six steps from takeoff for advanced vaulters.

for the athlete to move back 8 inches. This allows for accurate foot placement on the coach's mark, and no reaching for the board is necessary.

On the other hand, if the athlete is 8 inches behind the coach's mark and fouls by 8 inches, the problem is overstriding during the last 4 steps and at the end of the most critical point of the runway. The correct adjustment is for the athlete to move forward by 8 inches.

Remember that in a good runway, the stride length increases up through the penultimate stride. This lengthening should be very gradual and should never hinder acceleration or body posture. If the athlete reaches (lengthens stride) to hit the takeoff, this will cause deceleration and a postural leanback, destroying the chances for a good takeoff.

The distance to the board from the fourth or sixth step check mark is basically the average of the stride length during the latter portion of the run. Normally, for male jumpers running 10-count steps, this distance will be 30 to 32 feet, and for female jumpers running the same 10-count steps, the distance will be 28 to 30 feet.

A helpful hint is to periodically time the athlete over the last four steps from touchdown at the coach's mark to takeoff of the 10th step. This should be done first on the track without a board and again after moving back to the runway during a jump. The two sets of times should coordinate closely. This device can also be used to determine the most efficient runway length. The length that consistently provides the fastest times over the last four steps is obviously the length to use in competition. In some cases, a longer approach will not yield the fastest time over four strides because the athlete is not strong or mature enough to handle the extreme distance. It is better to be accelerating through the takeoff because any deceleration forces the athlete to lean back, taking him or her out of an effective jumping position. The count tempo setup is shown in Figure 2.3.

Summary

The approach is the most important concern for all jumping events. It alone dictates the success or failure of the entire jump. All the power, speed, impulse, and direction are developed during the approach run. Once airborne, other than controlling rotations, the athlete cannot contribute to the effectiveness of the jump. The athlete must be in contact with the ground to have any effect on the performance of a jump. For this reason, with the exception of the pole vault, more than 90% of the work should be directed at the runway approach.

Chapter 3
Strength and Power Development

It has long been recognized that an organism cannot develop unless it undergoes a period of overload training. For a muscle, a nerve, or an entire body to progress, it must be overloaded in one or all of the following ways:

- Increase the speed of performance
- Increase the total time of loading
- Increase the total load
- Increase the total number of performances

Different workloads affect the body differently, but a good rule of thumb is that to increase strength or endurance, you must increase the threshold by one third of normal activity. Depending on the goal, different functions and areas of the body respond to varied overload percentages.

Physiological Considerations

Hypertrophy (strength gain) occurs with regular overload activity. Strength gains are demonstrated through several physiological means within the muscle. Protein synthesis can only occur through bodily requirements in situations such as growth, injury, and overload training. All of these are dictated by the hormonal needs of the body.

As a coach, you should have some general knowledge about strength training. The challenge for coaches and athletes is to develop a training routine that causes hypertrophy of certain muscle types for special activities, especially those of a speed nature. Developing such a specialized routine is key for the jumping events.

> ## Coach's Tip
>
> **Progressive overload is the only means of achieving athletic development. Overload causes stress adaptation, which in turn causes improvement in strength, endurance, and technique.**

Intensity of exercise is the prime requisite of fast-twitch muscle development. Lifting moderate to heavy weights is the correct regimen for eliciting strength in fast-twitch muscle fiber.

The coach who is developing a strength training program must understand the way neurons stimulate the muscle. What happens in the nervous system is as important as what occurs in the muscle because it triggers activity in the individual muscles and muscle groups. We are interested in motor recruitment and how it eventually controls the muscle forces in each of the specific jump skills an athlete wishes to develop.

According to the "all or none" principle, a muscle-nerve unit will fire and contract at maximum effort or it will not fire and contract at all.

For a muscular skill to be at its highest level, as many muscle-nerve units as possible must be recruited. This is usually accomplished with loads rather than volume. A jumper seeks intensity during strength development, at times working at 80% to 100%. These submaximum to maximum loads are used during the final strength cycles.

During structured progressive training, a jumper can make sufficient improvements in strength. It may take months or even years, but this single developmental aspect contributes more to an athlete's success than any other training component. It improves skill technique, increases generation and utilization of speed during the runway, and also makes the athlete far less susceptible to injury.

In general, strength training has two primary goals: a peak speed of contraction and a peak load of contraction. Mechanically speaking, applied to performance, the two factors combined equal impulse (force × time). The development of impulse is the basis for all successful jumping.

A systematic approach to strength development must be thought out carefully for each athlete and adjusted somewhat as the athlete progresses through his or her career. However, regardless of the individual or the training level, there are common elements that must be integrated. These elements should follow standard order and training theory.

Early in the year, a general training regimen should provide stress to the working aerobic capacity of the body. In terms of weights, it would implement weight circuits of any varying nature. These weight circuits should in-

> ## Coach's Tip
>
> **Strength training is only a means of achieving success. It in itself is not an end product.**

volve activities that utilize the athlete's own body weight, such as interval training in any activity where the emphasis is on maximum repetitions of low intensity (35%-60%) with very short recovery intervals. The basic goal is cardiovascular activity that raises the oxidative capacities of the body.

Following the aerobic work, the goal should be muscle hypertrophy. Training should include any work that tends to increase muscle mass and muscle-nerve recruitment through moderate loads (50%-70% of 8-10 repetitions and gradually increasing the sets from three to six). This could be in the form of lifting weights but could also include work with a medicine ball, running, skipping, or bounding. By utilizing these dynamic activities in addition to lifting weights, much more balance and body awareness will be developed in this phase of strength training.

The next ingredient in the basic strength routine is the development of maximum strength. Maximum strength is best developed in the weight room using heavy free weights. Work in this area is very specific to the athlete's physical attributes, age, and skill level and should be closely monitored by the coach. The goal is to increase maximum dynamic strength. The sets should decrease to two or three, with repetitions limited to five.

At this point, the jumper is assumed to have reached a near-absolute strength peak for precompetition athletes. The strength developed is specific but will blend into later stages of training.

The next component of our training routine is power training. Power is the ability to maximize strength at the fastest possible rate and is probably the most important physical component for the jumper to develop. Our emphasis is on integrating power activities with strength activities. Power is best developed using a combination of ballistic body weight activity (plyometrics, etc.) and either Olympic or power lifts.

Olympic lifts include the clean and jerk, and the snatch. Olympic lifting is especially suited to developing explosive power and quickness in the athlete. Power lifting, on the other hand, includes the squat, the bench press, and the

dead lift. Because of the weight load used, this activity is characterized as slow strength movement. By complementing the Olympic lifts with power lifts and other dynamic activities, the result should be a jumper who is not only strong but can move with explosive quickness. This is the most important ingredient for proper preparation for jump training.

The final component of our plan is the speed emphasis phase. This phase is the link to incorporating a peak speed and a peak load force during the lifting and training sessions. The speed phase generally combines any of the speed activities (sprinting, bounding, skipping) with Olympic lifting (two to five repetitions at 80%-100% of maximum load) followed by power lifting (four to eight repetitions at or near 60% of maximum).

The speed emphasis phase should be followed by a recovery period that naturally follows the competitive season. This is generally characterized as an active rest period during which the athlete continues with informal and/or recreational activities. At the completion of the rest phase, the entire sequence begins again the next training year but at a more specific and higher workload.

Coach's Tip

In the total scheme of training, rest is as important as work.

Plyometrics Training

In our coaching vocabulary, *plyometrics* is a coined term for the elasticity component of strength training, which some coaches have come to view as a cure-all in strength training and event preparation. It is not. Plyometrics is simply a means of adding a strength and power development component to individual programs. Elastic strength training can be thought of as completing the chain of events that occurs in the athlete's total strength development package.

Muscles possess elasticity. During the stretching of a muscle, an automatic reflexive strengthening of the contraction occurs, which is referred to as the *myotonic reflex*.

Geoffrey Dyson (1977), in his book *Mechanics of Athletics*, describes the function of muscles during a loading phase: "The function of a muscle is simply to exert tension. This is best done when loaded sufficiently to lengthen despite trying to shorten. The faster it is allowed to shorten, the less tension it exerts; the faster it is forced to lengthen, the greater the tension." Dyson goes on to imply that too much stretch will cause a buckling effect. This results in an optimum load stimulus and will be counterproductive.

Plyometric muscle loading is accomplished in three ways:

1. Dropping down from a height to the ground, which forces a slight flexing of the legs.
2. Checking momentum with a plant leg in either a horizontal or vertical direction.
3. Increasing the load or tension by accelerating the free leg and/or the arms while the plant leg is undergoing amortization. This is referred to as *transference of force*.

The original concept of depth (or in-depth) training has created much confusion regarding the use of low boxes versus high boxes, downjumping, and how much training is good (or bad). Verhoshansky's (1967) original publications supported the theory that the greater the loading at prestretching, the greater the jumping results. As a result, many coaches came to believe that plyometrics was the only way to go in jump training. After all, they reasoned, if something is good, then more must be better. This has led to such foolhardy plyometric practices as athletes jumping off 8- and 12-foot platforms. Not surprisingly, plyometric training has been reported to be the

leading cause of soft tissue injury.

A coach and athlete should carefully consider strength, training level, age, and recovery in planning plyometric activities. The coach should look for specific work that will enhance strength and explosive power while developing the technical skills needed for the jumping events. Only then should plyometric activities be brought into the sequence of strength training. Stretch muscle training can and should be developed during ground-to-ground activities. Positive results have been reported about athletes such as Ulrike Meyfarth, who confines much of her training to 3-inch height platforms combined with ground-to-ground activities.

Skipping and rope jumping are excellent preparatory activities to incorporating the elasticity components of strength training.

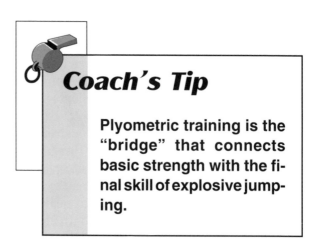

Coach's Tip

Plyometric training is the "bridge" that connects basic strength with the final skill of explosive jumping.

Training Principles

Plyometrics should be initiated early in the training year, during skill and technique development. All concepts and drills should be fully explained to athletes before they begin any activity. Plyometric jump training must follow a definite progression. Emphasis must be on proper execution of the activity rather than on the number of repetitions. When fatigued, the athlete must rest or stop the activity altogether. Improper performance in drills can lead to improper jump performances. The athlete should be trained to effectively apply force into the ground while running.

An athlete's plyometric needs are developed by two major training techniques. Short-distance, quick jumps are good for improving explosive power. Longer distance jumps improve muscle endurance and the development of takeoff timing for arms and legs. The minimum height for boxes used for jump training is 30 inches for short, explosive jumps and 43 inches for strength and power activity.

It is best to incorporate short-distance jump work the day before speed work. Even the mature athlete needs approximately 48 hours of recovery time before heading into another plyometric workout. Six to 8 days of rest are recommended prior to competition or long-distance jump training. Overload (weighted vests) training should not be used early in the season and not until the athlete completes strength evaluation tests. Overloading should begin during the absolute strength phase.

Training objectives should include proper foot placement: on the ball of the foot while running and flat on the foot while jumping. In both instances, the calf muscles should be sufficiently loaded so that the athlete can get onto and off the ground in the shortest possible time. Have the athlete attempt to transfer as much momentum as possible from the free limbs into the support leg. (The more force directed into the ground via the support leg, the more force delivered back into the jumper by the ground.) The objective is to combine the forces generated by the support leg with additional forces provided by the swinging arms and free leg into one instantaneous reaction against the ground. The speed at which muscle fibers are forced to lengthen has a direct bearing on the resultant force.

Strength Evaluation

A certain sequence of activities should be followed in plyometric training to prevent injuries and properly design load progressions. Strength evaluation is probably not necessary before beginning light plyometrics early in the season. Low-impact activities such as rope jumping, skipping, and postural bounding drills should not cause extreme fatigue or injury. However, before prescribing high-impact activities, the coach should evaluate the athlete's strength to determine the correct volume and intensity for load progressions. The athlete must be strong enough to work through the plyometric activities and be able to recover before moving into subsequent training sessions.

Two specific strength indexes should be addressed by the coach before allowing an athlete to participate in high-impact jumping or bounding activities: balance and static strength and strength response.

To evaluate balance and static strength, the athlete should do a one-leg squat, ending in a standing position. An even better test is for the athlete to quarter squat two times his or her body weight (see Figure 3.1). Either or both of these tests should be completed before the athlete does any high-impact jumping or bounding. If these skills cannot be accomplished with relative ease, the athlete's strength is insufficient to safely perform plyometric activities.

An alternate-leg five-step hop test is the best way to evaluate strength response. From a standing position, the athlete should do five continuous bounds on a single leg (see Figure 3.2) and then do the same thing on the other leg. The distances should be the same for both legs. If that isn't the case, the weak leg should be strengthened before high-level single-leg activities are attempted. A weak leg is a major cause of injury for both runners and jumpers. For some athletes, a month will take care of deficiencies in one or both legs. Other athletes may take a year or more to reach desired strength levels. These athletes must be brought along gradually before starting any high-stress activities.

A coach should evaluate an athlete's strength in terms of the requirements for different events to determine whether to emphasize stretch reflex or maximum strength. For some athletes, a cycle or even a year may need to be devoted specifically to increasing strength. Elite jumpers require great amounts of eccentric and concentric strength. During a high jump takeoff, four to five times the body's weight is exerted through the takeoff leg into the ground. Similarly, the long jumper will exert a little over 10 times his or her body weight during takeoff, and the triple jumper exerts nearly 12 times his

Figure 3.1   Tests to evaluate balance-static strength: (a) quarter squat using resistance equaling two times body weight; (b) standing single-leg squat with return to standing position. This is to be completed free standing with arms used only for balance.

Figure 3.2   Five-step single-leg hop test. After completing this test with the right leg, measure the distance from standing right foot placement to final landing spot of right foot. Repeat the test on the left foot and measure distance. The goal is to have the right and left feet test the same. It may take a while to achieve equal strength in both legs.

or her body weight (which is probably why it takes so long to develop a world-class triple jumper). This underscores why so much emphasis must be placed on jump strength activities.

Progression of Plyometric Drills

Experience has shown that all jump strength training should be sequential, progressing from the simple, low-impact activities to the more complicated and stressful drills. The following sequence of activities corresponds to the activities that appear in the subsequent strength training program for jumpers.

Rope Jumping. This is a relatively low-impact, high-energy activity. It is good to begin rope jumping in the summer and to increase speed and repetitions gradually.

Lateral Bench Hops. This is an excellent drill for body awareness, arm-leg timing, and explosive power. It is used during *every* strength training session and also as a test to evaluate power three times a year. The athlete stands alongside a weight bench or 16- to 20-inch-high box and double-leg hops to the opposite side of the bench or box and back (see Figure 3.3). The goal is to complete as many ground contacts as possible on both sides of the bench/box in 20 seconds.

Five-Step Hopping (Single Leg). This drill can be used as a training device as well as to evaluate balance, as described earlier. The idea is to balance repetitions of five bounds on each leg.

Standing (Single Leg). To learn this drill, the athlete bounds in place using both arms and placing all emphasis on the ground support leg. If done properly, the support leg will provide the power off the ground and the heel will come to the buttocks on each repetition. The athlete should not move to the next sequence until this drill can be completed 20 times equally well on both legs.

Single-Leg Bounds for Distance. This is similar to the single-leg in-place drill except that the athlete covers distance, doing either maximum repetitions or a specific number of repetitions (see Figure 3.4). For example, the athlete makes 14 ground contacts on the left followed by 14 on the right times four sets. Progressively greater distance should be covered on each set. This drill provides the highest intensity when the athlete is most fatigued.

RR-LL Bounding. This drill increases the skill level over single-leg bounds. The athlete (in motion) makes two ground contacts on the right leg followed by two ground contacts on the left leg (up to 30-100 meters).

Double-Leg Bounds. This activity is done using boxes and/or hurdles. The athlete begins by stepping off a box and landing on both feet, then immediately jumps over a hurdle or up onto another box (see Figure 3.5). This drill can be done with either low or high repetitions. An alternative to this drill would be single-leg box

Figure 3.3 Lateral bench hops.

Figure 3.4 Single-leg bounds.

Figure 3.5 Double-leg bounds.

Figure 3.6 Low step-up/step-down with weights.

or hurdle bounds at various heights (low for beginners).

Speed Bounds. This drill is generally used over short distances (20-40 meters). The athlete should concentrate on making a specified number of ground contacts. Early sessions should begin with 16 ground contacts, with the athlete progressing to 12 contacts for maximum speed late in the season. Speed bounding should be used in preparing for major competitions where speed is more important than power.

Assisted or Downhill Training. This training system can be used throughout the preparation and competition seasons. An area with a slight decline and good footing should be selected and used throughout the year. The idea is to run down the hill, forcing a high leg turnover and a longer than normal stride length (not reaching). The athlete should run at a constant three-quarter effort (never more). The goal of this activity is to improve posture, leg recovery, and foot placement under the hips. The athlete should run 8 to 12 repetitions of 40 to 60 meters. As the season progresses, the athlete becomes more and more efficient. This exercise stretches the hamstrings and forces rapid leg turnover, enhancing both strength and speed. An alternative to downhill running is to run a downhill runway and incorporate a penulti-mate and a jump takeoff.

Low Step-Up/Step-Down With Weights. This drill should be used at the completion of the power phase of the athlete's lifting cycle. A 6-inch box should be placed in the power lifting rack. Using a full bar and weights, the athlete steps (single leg) onto and off the box (see Figure 3.6). The athlete should begin with a load equal to his or her body weight (doing three to four repetitions) and gradually progress to three times that weight. This is a long-term exercise, and the athlete should not attempt to lift too much weight too soon.

Planning Training Programs for Jumpers

There are several phases that comprise the athlete's training program. Moving from the overall program down to the daily training session, these phases are:

- *Macrocycle.* The prefix *macro* means large, so this cycle would encompass our entire long-range training program. It might be a 5-year program, but most likely refers to a yearly training plan.
- *Mesocycle.* This term refers to a group of smaller training units. In some cases, the unit would last several weeks and would have a specific set of goals. It might be a unit in which aerobic activity is the major emphasis, or it might encompass special activities such as overload plyometrics. Sometimes a coach might want to limit a unit to half a mesocycle; that is, if a mesocycle is set for 6 weeks, a particular activity might be emphasized for only 3 weeks.
- *Microcycle.* This term is specific to small units. In most instances, a unit would last from a week to 10 days. This is shown in the weekly workouts included at the end of each specific event chapter.
- *Session.* For most purposes, a session is one training unit. If an athlete trains only once per day, it indicates one session. Sometime a coach prescribes a two-unit session each day, and in extreme instances, three sessions a day.

The yearly macrocycle for jumpers can be broken down into six mesocycles:

1. General preparation (4 weeks)
2. Special preparation (6 weeks)
3. Power development (3 weeks)
4. Preparation for indoor competition (4 weeks)
5. Power development (3 weeks)
6. Preparation for outdoor competition (4 weeks)

This program is designed to achieve a peak performance indoors and then an absolute peak during the outdoor championships.

Planned performance training is the only guaranteed means of achieving success at a particular time. It is important that the athlete achieve his or her best performance at the right time. For example, the high school athlete's ultimate performance should occur during the state championships and the elite athlete's during the World Championships or the Olympic Games.

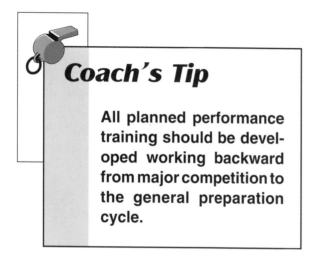

Coach's Tip

All planned performance training should be developed working backward from major competition to the general preparation cycle.

Peaking at the desired time is not a matter of luck. It comes only through deliberate, planned preparation that entails a step-by-step physiological, psychological, and competitive set of progressive activities.

For many years, athletes were trained at or near their maximum potential for as long as their bodies could tolerate. We now know that loads, duration, and intensity must be mixed and matched. For example, when volume increases, intensity must decrease.

With any type of training, the body responds to stress by adapting to it. In fact, the adaptation is a new compensation, better known as *supercompensation*. Note on Figure 3.7 that recovery or rest must precede supercompensation. That means setting a high priority on the interruption of all types of training with proper amounts of rest to allow the body to recover before assuming additional stress.

General Preparation

The general preparation phase is designed to place the athlete at a moderate level of fitness. Early in this phase, the primary emphasis is on aerobic conditioning and later shifts to aerobic power. General strength conditioning for all athletes is initiated using a low load with 10 to 12 repetitions. Figure 3.8 is a sample program for the general preparation phase.

At the end of this phase, each athlete is tested with a single-leg five-hop test, a standing long jump, a standing triple jump, an overhead shot put, a lateral bench hop for 20 seconds, a 30-meter sprint, and a 3-mile run.

The left-hand column of Figure 3.8 lists activities and indicates the areas of emphasis during each mesocycle. To the right are the actual description, volume, and duration of each activity. For strength training activity occurring after the general preparation phase, all weights are determined by a maximum two-repetition

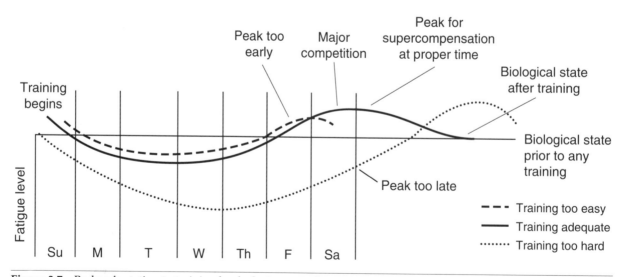

Figure 3.7   Body adaptation to training loads during a week.

test at the end of each cycle. This is indicated by the "Test for max" entry. As the athlete moves into the new mesocycle, all lifting activities are prescribed by a percentage figure. For example, during the special preparation cycle, an athlete completes a power clean lift of 250 pounds × 2 repetitions. He shows a maximum lift of 250 pounds. During the power development cycle, the power clean is prescribed to be done at 70%. The athlete looks at Table 3.1 and sees that 70% of 250 pounds is 175 pounds. Thus, all lifts are based on a percentage of the previous cycle's next max test (see Table 3.1, p. 38).

At the bottom of each workout is a legend of work-to-rest ratios. Keeping in mind that each individual athlete may have a different workload, various activities must be followed by some type of recovery. Some activities require more rest than others, and some activities supplement others. It is important to consider the particular workload level of each athlete when prescribing a train-recover ratio for each mesocycle.

"Training" indicates stress response training and usually represents at least a moderate workload. "Active rest" refers to some type of activity that is usually not as demanding as the sport-specific training activities. In the power development phase, "power program" is used to denote intense training. This type of program can only occur twice a week and should be followed by a lengthy rest period such as a school holiday break. Competitions are usually preceded by a rest day. Finally, "skill" refers to a filming session or simulated competition and should also be preceded by a rest day.

Special Preparation

The special preparation mesocycle has an established goal of identifying "special needs": the development of aerobic power through tempo runs of 100 to 300 meters or the application of effective force while running as developed in uphill runs. In addition, much time is spent on the development of technique or form running (see Figure 3.9).

For this mesocycle, strength training loads have been increased to 70% to 80% with a transition of volume of 5 to 10 repetitions.

Specific body areas and lifts are identified and taught. The strength training includes Thursday and Sunday sessions using like percentages and lifts, but the Tuesday session is more jump-specific with more loading and more specialization in activity.

Strength-speed training is an attempt to blend the power activities of plyometrics with the running activities. There is a lot of emphasis on the technical aspects because this is the period when major changes must be made in the athlete's preparation technique. In fact, major changes in technique should never be made after this period.

Power Development

The power development phase is best described as a maximum volume and load cycle. If performed properly, it takes the athlete to his or her limit of fatigue tolerance. Recall that fatigue must be followed by a rest unit. In this instance, 2 or 3 days will not allow sufficient recovery. Thus, we place this phase just before Christmas vacation, when all athletes are likely to be far less active than usual.

The real emphasis of the cycle occurs in the Sunday and Thursday strength sessions (see Figure 3.10). Not only are there fairly high repetitions and percentages, but activities are "supersetted"; that is, a half-squat exercise is followed by another half-squat exercise of even greater intensity, which is followed by a more intense bounding activity. Then the athlete immediately moves to a prone leg press, which is repeated twice and followed by more bounding. All of this is accomplished before the athlete moves on to upper body work. Such extremely intense activity is not recommended for the young jumper; however, this system could be adapted for younger athletes. This emphasis on maximum weight is the optimal load concept, which is used to produce faster movement response. Lifting should be interspersed with two plyometrics sessions a week.

Note that after Christmas vacation, the athlete will exhibit the highest strength and explosive capabilities of his or her career. This is due to the supercompensation principle.

General Preparation Phase

Activities	Drills
Running	30-min runs or Fartlek (one-half mesocycle)
	Extensive tempo, long intervals—medium recovery or short intervals; very short recovery 35.70% (one-half mesocycle)
	Intensive aerobic power: 80%-89% hills or flat
	Speed: 80 m, 90%-100%
Strength Muscle balance	Body weight circuits: one-half of mesocycle (full squats)
Develop tendon ends	Cleans (3 × 10), high step-ups (3 × 15), quads (3 × 15), hamstring curls (3 × 15 × 1-day week/negative [extend with loaded curl]), incline bench (3 × 15), dumbbells (3 × 25)
	Test for max—last day of mesocycle; goal is range of movement; 10 reps for all or none, three units/week (all); only difference is two sessions may be better than one
Strength and Speed Power, strength Dynamic balance	For meso endurance (one-half mesocycle): • Lateral bench hops (2 × 20 s); to be completed on strength days • Double leg (20-40 m/set); progress double to single • RR–LL (single, flat and stadium stairs) • Backward hopping (one-half mesocycle)
	For meso power, 6-10 reps/set (with weighted vest) of the following: • Depth jumps • Hurdle hops • Longer jumps
Technical	Changes in event
	Short run approaches (acceleration curve)
	Work last two steps
	Form running
	Video analysis
Multithrows	For meso endurance (one-half mesocycle): • Light medicine ball for strength endurance
	For meso strength (one-half mesocycle): • Heavy implement throwing and drills • Heavy medicine ball work (two sessions/week)
Flexibility	Static testing
	Static stretching

(continued)

Figure 3.8 Sample 4-week general preparation mesocycle.

Activities	Drills
Cooperation	General • Games: Basketball, badminton, volleyball, soccer Specific • Standing triple jump, lateral bench hops, sprints, hurdle drills
Psychological	Educate in: skills; power lifting; multihops, multithrows, technique, film study, motivation

Legend of Work-to-Rest Ratios

week 1

Monday	Tuesday	Wednesday	Thursday	Friday	Saturday	Sunday
Train	Active rest	Train	Active rest	Train	Rest	Train

week 2

Monday	Tuesday	Wednesday	Thursday	Friday	Saturday	Sunday
Train	Train	Rest	Train	Active rest	Rest	Train

week 3

Monday	Tuesday	Wednesday	Thursday	Friday	Saturday	Sunday
Train	Train	Active rest	Train	Rest	Rest	Train

week 4

Monday	Tuesday	Wednesday	Thursday	Friday	Saturday	Sunday
Train	Train	Rest	Train	Train	Rest	Train

Figure 3.8   *(continued)*

Special Preparation Phase

Activities	Drills
Running	Speed (runways)
	Speed endurance
	Aerobic power: 2/week
	Sprint drills: 2/week
	Power speed (hills, stadium stairs): 1 each, 2/week
Strength	On Thursday, Sunday:
	• Cleans: 3 × 5, 1 × 10 @ 70%
	• 1/2 squats: 3 × 5, 1 × 10 @ 70%
	• Hamstrings: 3 × 5, 1 × 10 @ 70%
	• Dumbbells (arm action): 3 × 10 @ 80%
	• Incline press: 3 × 5, 1 × 10 @ 70%
	Tuesday
	• Clean and jerk: 2 × 3 @ 80%, 2 × 2 @ 85%, 1 × 3 @ 90%
	• Inverted leg press: 3 × 8 @ 80%
	• Hamstrings: 3 × 8 @ 80% (single)
	• Snatch: 3 × 5 @ 70%
	• Low step-ups: 2 × 3 @ 80%, 2 × 5 @ 80%
	• Increase 0/0 × 2, 5 each week
	• Test for max
Strength and Speed	For meso power (one-half mesocycle):
	• Standing one-step, two-step triple jumps
	• All half-approach, full-approach jumping
	• Box jumping
	• Lateral bench hops
	• Hurdle hops
	• Depth jumps
	• Depth to hurdles (no weight)
	For meso endurance (one-half mesocycle):
	• Longer jumps, 3-4 sets (while outdoors)
Technical	Full run approaches
	Drills specific for pole vault
	Jump for height (film evaluation)
Multithrows	Medicine balls and varied implements (medium weight)
	Decreasing volume, increased intensity
Flexibility	Static
	Dynamic (i.e., sprint-hurdle drills)
Coordination	Event-specific drills
Psychological	Dedication, persistence, concentration

(continued)

Figure 3.9 Sample 6-week special preparation mesocycle.

Legend of Work-to-Rest Ratios

week 1

Monday	Tuesday	Wednesday	Thursday	Friday	Saturday	Sunday
Train	Train	Train	Active rest	Train	Train	Rest

week 2

Monday	Tuesday	Wednesday	Thursday	Friday	Saturday	Sunday
Train	Train	Train	Active rest	Train	Train	Rest

week 3

Monday	Tuesday	Wednesday	Thursday	Friday	Saturday	Sunday
Active rest	Train	Active rest	Train	Train	Train	Rest

week 4

Monday	Tuesday	Wednesday	Thursday	Friday	Saturday	Sunday
Train	Train	Train	Train	Active Rest	Rest	Rest

week 5

Monday	Tuesday	Wednesday	Thursday	Friday	Saturday	Sunday
Train	Train	Rest	Train	Rest	Train	Rest

week 6

Monday	Tuesday	Wednesday	Thursday	Friday	Saturday	Sunday
Train	Train	Rest	Train	Train	Active rest	Rest

Figure 3.9 *(continued)*

Power Development Phase

Activities	Drills
Running	For speed and power: • Stadium stairs • Hill sprints (drop down) • Belt sprint (for leg speed) • Sprint-hurdle drills (daily) For special endurance: • 200-300 80%-90% • 150s 90%-100% • 80s 90%-100%
Strength and Power Jumps	On the first and third days: • Half squats/set × 6 reps @ 80% • Half squats/set × 8 reps @ 90% • Single-leg hops to 40 each leg • Inverted-leg press/set × 5 @ 100% of half squat • Inverted-leg press/set × 4 @ 110% of half squat • 8 × stair hops, single leg each flight • Power clean/set × 8 @ 70% • Power clean/set × 10 @ 60% • Depth jump over hurdle × 15 • Snatch/set × 4 @ 90% On the second day: • Cleans: 3 × 5, 1 × 10 @ 70% • Half squats: 3 × 4, 1 × 10 @ 70% • High step-ups: 2 × 16 @ 85% • Hamstrings: 3 × 5 @ 70%, 2 × 8 @ 75% • Low step-ups and down: 1 × 8 @ 70%, 1 × 8 @ 75%, 1 x 8 @ 90% Max weight test
Technical	Consistency of runway Speed for last six steps Consistency of height over 8-10 jumps
Multithrows	Meso power (step throw)
Flexibility	Static stretching
Psychological	Intensity of power workouts; concentration on consistency

(continued)

Figure 3.10   Sample 3-week power development mesocycle.

Legend of Work-to-Rest Ratios

week 1

Monday	Tuesday	Wednesday	Thursday	Friday	Saturday	Sunday
Train	Train	Active rest	Power program	Train	Rest	Power program

week 2

Monday	Tuesday	Wednesday	Thursday	Friday	Saturday	Sunday
Train	Active rest	Active rest	Power program	Train	Rest	Power program

week 3

Monday	Tuesday	Wednesday	Thursday	Friday	Saturday	Sunday
Train	Active rest	Active rest	Power program	Train	Rest	Power program

Figure 3.10   *(continued)*

Indoor Competition Phase

Activities	Drills
Running	Sprint-hurdle drills (daily)
	Power-bound/power-sprint
	20-40-20 speed
	80s curve or straight 90%-100%
	Power sprints 100%
	100-150s 90%-100%
Strength	One-half meso: absolute strength maintenance—specific strength
	Power: Tuesday and Sunday or Tuesday and Thursday, 2 sessions/week • Snatch: 1 x 6 @ 80% • Half squats: 1 x 6 @ 70%, 1 x 5 @ 80%, 1 x 4 @ 85% • Hamstrings: 1 x 6 @ 70%, 1 x 5 @ 80%, 1 x 4 @ 85% • Lateral bench hops: 1 x 20 s • Cleans: 1 x 6 @ 70%, 1 x 5 @ 80%, 1 x 4 @ 85%
	One-half meso: • Max or near-max lift, 1 every 14 days or less
Strength-Speed	Full approach or skill drills • Speed bounding • Depth jump, low variety • Short jumps • Lightweight implement throwing
Technical	Competition-specific • Full jumps, film evaluation, problem solving or throws
Flexibility	Static stretching, proprioceptive neuromuscular facilitation (PNF) stretches
Psychological	Confidence, concentration

(continued)

Figure 3.11   Sample 4-week indoor competition mesocycle.

Legend of Work-to-Rest Ratios

week 1

Monday	Tuesday	Wednesday	Thursday	Friday	Saturday	Sunday
Train	*Train*	*Rest*	*Skill*	*Train*	*Competition*	*Rest*

week 2

Monday	Tuesday	Wednesday	Thursday	Friday	Saturday	Sunday
Train	*Train*	*Rest*	*Train*	*Rest*	*Competition*	*Rest*

week 3

Monday	Tuesday	Wednesday	Thursday	Friday	Saturday	Sunday
Train	*Train*	*Rest*	*Train*	*Rest*	*Rest or competition*	*Rest*

week 4

Monday	Tuesday	Wednesday	Thursday	Friday	Saturday	Sunday
Train	*Train*	*Rest*	*Rest*	*Competition*	*Competition*	*Rest*

Figure 3.11   *(continued)*

Outdoor Competition Phase

Activities	Drills
Running	Speed (special endurance)
Strength	**One-half meso—two sessions/week:**
	Day 1
	• Snatches: 1 × 6 @ 70%, 1 × 4 @ 80%
	• Hamstrings: 1 × 6 @ 70%, 1 × 5 @ 80%, 1 × 4 @ 85%
	• Lateral bench hops with dumbbells: 1 × 12 s
	• Cleans: 1 × 6 @ 70%, 1 × 5 @ 80%, 1 × 4 @ 85%
	Day 2
	• Quarter squats: 1 × 6 @ 70%, 1 × 4 @ 85%
	• Low step-ups: 1 × 8 @ 70%, 1 × 6 @ 75%, 1 × 6 @ 80%
	• Hamstrings: 1 × 5 @ 75%, 1 × 4 @ 85%
	• Lateral bench hops (light): 1 × 15
	• Cleans: 1 × 6 @ 75%, 1 × 4 @ 85%
	One-half meso—one session/week:
	• Cleans: 1 × 6 @ 70%, 1 × 5 @ 80%, 1 × 4 @ 85%
	• Quarter squats: 1 × 6 @ 70%, 1 × 5 @ 80%, 1 × 4 @ 85%
	• Hamstrings: 1 × 8 @ 70%, 1 × 6 @ 75%, 1 × 6 @ 80%
	• Lateral bench hops: 1 × 12 @ 100% (light)
	10 Days Prior to Major Competition
	• Quarter-squat cleans: 1 × 4 @ 70%, 1 × 2 @ 85%, 1 × 1 @ 90%-100%
Strength and Speed	Jumps specific to event
	High intensity/low volume
Technical	Competitive analysis
Multithrows	Low volume/high intensity
	Light implements
Flexibility	Some static, mostly dynamic
Psychological	Confidence

(continued)

Figure 3.12   Sample 4-week outdoor competition mesocycle.

Legend of Work-to-Rest Ratios

week 1

Monday	Tuesday	Wednesday	Thursday	Friday	Saturday	Sunday
Skill or train	Train	Rest	Active rest	Rest	Competition	Rest

week 2

Monday	Tuesday	Wednesday	Thursday	Friday	Saturday	Sunday
Skill or train	Train	Train	Active rest	Rest	Train	Rest

week 3

Monday	Tuesday	Wednesday	Thursday	Friday	Saturday	Sunday
Skill or train	Active rest	Rest	Competition	Rest	Competition	Rest

Figure 3.12   *(continued)*

Table 3.1
Weight Training Percentage

Wt.	40%	45%	50%	55%	60%	65%	70%	75%	80%	85%	90%	95%
50	20	25	25	30	30	35	35	40	40	45	45	45
60	25	30	30	35	35	40	40	45	50	55	55	55
70	30	35	35	40	40	50	50	55	55	60	60	65
80	30	40	45	50	50	55	60	65	70	70	75	
90	35	40	45	50	55	60	65	65	75	80	80	85
100	40	45	50	55	60	65	70	75	80	85	90	95
110	45	50	55	60	65	70	75	85	90	95	100	105
120	50	55	60	65	70	80	85	90	95	100	110	115
130	55	60	65	70	80	85	90	100	105	110	115	125
140	55	65	70	75	85	90	100	105	110	120	125	135
150	60	70	75	85	90	100	105	115	120	130	135	145
160	65	75	80	90	95	105	110	120	130	135	145	150
170	70	80	85	95	100	110	120	125	135	145	155	160
180	70	80	90	100	110	115	125	135	145	155	160	170
190	75	85	90	105	115	125	135	145	150	160	170	180
200	80	90	100	110	120	130	140	150	160	170	180	190
210	85	100	105	115	125	135	145	155	170	180	190	190
220	90	100	110	120	130	145	155	165	175	185	200	210
230	95	108	115	125	140	150	160	175	185	195	205	220
240	95	110	120	130	145	155	170	180	190	205	215	230
250	100	115	125	140	150	165	175	190	200	215	225	240
260	105	120	130	145	155	170	180	195	210	220	235	245
270	110	125	135	150	160	175	190	200	215	230	245	255
280	110	125	140	155	170	180	195	210	225	240	250	265
290	115	130	145	160	175	190	205	220	230	245	260	270
300	120	135	150	165	180	195	210	225	240	255	270	285
310	125	140	155	170	185	200	215	230	250	265	280	295
320	130	145	160	175	190	210	225	240	255	270	290	305
330	135	150	165	180	200	210	230	250	265	280	300	315
350	145	160	175	195	210	230	245	265	280	300	315	335
360	140	160	190	200	220	230	250	270	290	310	320	340
390	160	180	200	210	230	250	270	290	310	330	350	370
420	170	190	210	230	250	270	290	320	340	360	380	400
450	180	200	230	250	270	290	320	340	360	380	410	430
480	190	220	240	260	290	310	340	360	380	410	430	460
510	200	230	260	280	310	330	360	380	410	430	460	490
540	220	240	270	300	320	350	380	410	430	460	490	510
570	230	260	290	310	340	370	400	430	460	480	510	540
600	240	270	300	330	360	390	420	450	480	510	540	570

Rounded to 5 lb.

A second power development phase can be used as a transition between the indoor and outdoor competition mesocycles.

Preparation for Indoor Competition

The indoor preparation phase should also be considered the preparation phase for high school or nonindoor competitors. Outdoor preparation precludes strength activities for those college programs that consist of both indoor and outdoor seasons.

Coach's Tip

When entering into the competition phase, the coach and athlete should remember that "the hay is in the barn." The preliminary work is complete. The goal now is simply performance.

The purpose of this phase is to reduce the volume of training and begin special speed activities. The intent is not to promote a backing off attitude toward training but to temper or moderate activities, particularly the strength training. Note that the load percentages range from 70% to 85% but there are fewer repetitions (see Figure 3.11).

The bounding activities have changed from power to speed. Basically, the jumper's emphasis has now moved from strength development to maintenance, and the real priority is to move toward competition.

Preparation for Outdoor Competition

The competition phase is perhaps the most complex for the coach to prescribe because the individual athletes' idiosyncrasies must be understood and their abilities assessed accurately to plan the activity immediately preceding competition. Some respond well to rest and some do not. Too often we intensify activity, and this is detrimental to the nerve recruitment properties that are necessary for high performances.

The goal of this phase is to maintain strength levels yet provide sufficient recoveries (see Figure 3.12). All activity is performed at a moderate load with few repetitions.

Ten days prior to a major competition, we want the athlete to complete the final strength work at a moderate level for a single maximum-type activity. Everything should be performed at near top speed and with maximum recovery periods. The only concern is achieving high performance. There should be no technical changes. Confidence is the key—the athlete is ready to perform well, and he or she knows it.

Summary

Several physiological considerations must be addressed when designing a strength and power program for jumpers. Training drills and activities must follow a progression that safely increases the athlete's workload, speed, and overall performance. A plyometrics program can assist in evaluating and improving the athlete's strength and speed. A comprehensive training program includes both general and specific preparation phases, power development, and preparation for competition. Together these components comprise a well-rounded training program that will foster improvements in the four jumping events.

Part II | Event-Specific Technique and Training

When an athlete evolves to a point where he or she is ready to specialize in a particular event, it's like going through a graduation commencement exercise. The days of general participation are gone—not forgotten, but gone. A whole new era begins. To become an event specialist, an athlete must fully understand his or her personal strengths and weaknesses and, more important, must learn how to capitalize on the strong points and improve the weak points. To be successful, athletes must understand themselves to the fullest.

The role of the coach in working with an event specialist is almost awesome. The coach must be teacher, counselor, and ultimately partner to the athlete. Successes and failures must be shared. However, the important thing to remember is that the product, the athlete's performance level, is a direct result of the process. The process may be short or long term, but choices and decisions must be made early on.

Event preparation must be centered around specific tasks, and both coach and athlete must focus all their energies on those tasks. Recall that four mechanical factors govern all of the jumping events. These factors have to do with height, angle, speed, and rotations at takeoff, and they do not change from event to event. Now, however, these factors must be looked at in terms of fine-tuning the skills of a particular athlete to achieve peak performance in a particular event. The coach and the athlete must break down the event into its constituent parts and set goals for each individual segment, one at a time, eventually blending them back into a unified whole.

Although governed by physics, style must be selected to suit a particular athlete. Decisions must be made regarding the length of the runway. Is there too much speed to make the transition into the takeoff? What landing should be used for the long and triple jumps? Is a double-arm or single-arm motion more effective for the athlete's specific event? What body posture prevents or speeds rotations? What method of approach run start will best suit the athlete? The list is endless, but over time, through experiment, analysis, and application of the basic mechanical laws, the athlete can achieve great success in the specific area.

Chapter 4 examines the long jump. The triple and high jumps are explored in chapters 5 and 6, respectively. Chapter 7 delves into the pole vault.

Chapter 4
Long Jump

The long jump is the most neglected jumping event. Too few coaches teach and monitor correct jumping technique, just as too few athletes really work at the event. It's as if everyone assumes that the fastest athlete will be the best long jumper. Although relatively simple, the long jump should be broken into components that can be developed individually. These ingredients are the keys to the effectiveness of the total long jump.

Keys to Long Jumping

- Achieve maximum speed in the approach

- Lower the hips in the penultimate stride and allow them to rise to maximum height at takeoff while maintaining speed

- Move the hips forward and up for maximum distance from board contact to foot release

- Prevent or neutralize forward rotation during flight

- Position the feet horizontally at maximum distance from the hips at landing

Approach

An athlete who is fast and can conserve this velocity throughout the takeoff will be a good long jumper. Horizontal velocity in the long jump contributes more than two times the potential distance to the total jump than does vertical velocity. As mentioned in chapter 1, the elite long jumper will leave the board at an angle of 20° or less. The faster the velocity, the higher and longer the center-of-mass trajectory.

Ideally, the jumper will accelerate from the start to the finish of the approach. Acceleration is demonstrated by two distinct factors: an increase in stride length and an increase in stride frequency. Anything that causes the athlete to reduce stride length and thus to decelerate will result in an inferior jump. Therefore, the jumper's approach to the board at optimal stride length is a major factor in long jump performance.

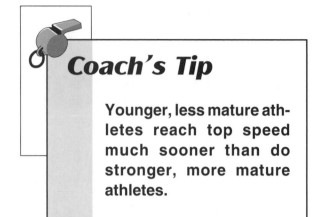

Coach's Tip

Younger, less mature athletes reach top speed much sooner than do stronger, more mature athletes.

Posture Through Acceleration

Body posture during the first six to eight strides is one problem area. If the jumper pushes out hard from the takeoff mark and does not allow the body to gradually reach an upright position, the stride length will either shorten or

Mike Powell

This sequence details the entire takeoff through landing of Mike Powell's world record perfor- Of special interest is the directional path of his center of mass, which shows a lowering 11.1 meters per second. It is unclear why his best jump was produced by such a relatively slow

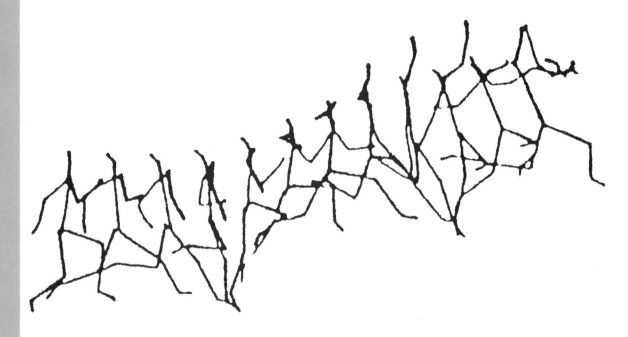

lengthen in an irregular manner. As mentioned in other chapters, body posture must be a product of acceleration.

As always, the most effective and efficient position for velocity is to be upright and tall. At the onset of acceleration, there is a pronounced forward lean, then gradually, as speed reaches the maximum, the body will naturally assume a tall, upright posture (see Figure 4.1). For a mature long jumper, this erect position should be reached in the first 12 to 14 strides.

Length of the Runway

The length of the approach run is determined by how long it takes the athlete to reach top speed. The elite athlete will generally reach top speed in approximately 20 to 22 strides; the developing athlete will reach this ultimate speed in 16 to 18 strides. The coach and the

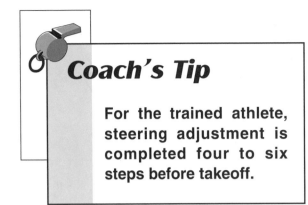

Coach's Tip

For the trained athlete, steering adjustment is completed four to six steps before takeoff.

athlete can best determine this distance on the track and away from the runway. Only after the athlete has demonstrated an optimum length for an approach run should it be incorporated onto the actual runway. Remember that the sole purpose of the runway is for the athlete to reach the takeoff point at the fastest possible velocity. The basic rule to follow is: *Set the*

mance of 8.95 meters (29 feet 4-1/2 inches) at the 1991 World Championships in Japan. accompanied by maximum hip height at takeoff. This jump occurred with a velocity of speed. Perhaps more time was gained from ground takeoff to foot release.

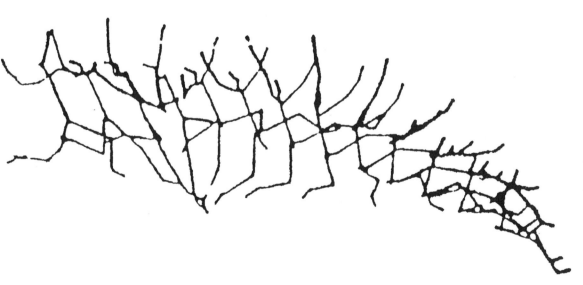

Note. Used with permission of Baseball Magazine Sha Co., Ltd.

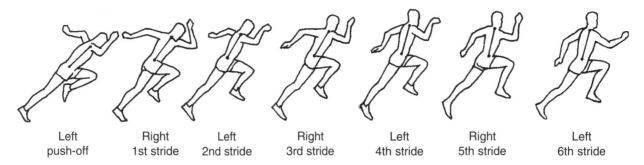

Left push-off	Right 1st stride	Left 2nd stride	Right 3rd stride	Left 4th stride	Right 5th stride	Left 6th stride

Figure 4.1   Body posture during the first six strides of the long jump.

Table 4.1
Mike Powell's Stride Length at 1990 TAC Championships in Norwalk, CA

Order of strides	Strides remaining before takeoff	1 (7.95)	2 (8.13)	3 (7.95)	4 (F)	5 (F)	6 (8.24)	Average
		Trial No. (official distance of jump in meters)						
1	23	0.72	0.75	0.68	0.76	0.90	0.74	0.76
2	22	0.90	0.85	0.90	0.98	1.07	0.96	0.94
3	21	1.57	1.57	1.59	1.41	1.56	1.56	1.54
4	20	1.62	1.60	1.66	1.65	1.73	1.62	1.65
5	19	1.88	2.02	2.01	1.90	2.12	1.89	1.97
6	18	1.99	2.00	1.99	2.10	2.15	2.09	2.05
7	17	2.18	2.17	2.24	2.27	2.24	2.18	2.21
8	16	2.20	2.25	2.28	2.35	2.28	2.22	2.26
9	15	2.35	2.28	2.33	2.30	2.35	2.32	2.32
10	14	2.35	2.41	2.29	2.43	2.44	2.33	2.37
11	13	2.37	2.42	2.31	2.33	2.41	2.35	2.36
12	12	2.41	2.44	2.50	2.45	2.53	2.37	2.45
13	11	2.51	2.47	2.46	2.50	2.48	2.47	2.48
14	10	2.49	2.51	2.45	2.45	2.46	2.44	2.46
15	9	2.42	2.52	2.58	2.35	2.58	2.73	2.53
16	8	2.42	2.50	2.48	2.62	2.48	2.51	2.50
17	7	2.72	2.59	2.61	2.60	2.60	2.26	2.56
18	6	2.47	2.44	2.47	2.48	2.54	2.41	2.47
19	5	2.70	2.63	2.55	2.53	2.35	2.70	2.57
20	4	2.66	2.50	2.48	2.42	2.30	2.72	2.51
21	3	2.33	2.37	2.43	2.49	2.22	2.48	2.39
22	2	2.31	2.31	2.35	2.36	2.28	2.41	2.34
23	1	2.20	2.18	2.11	2.14	2.04	2.16	2.14

Note. Used with permission of Dr. James Hay.

runway to fit the individual's acceleration curve; the acceleration curve should not be dictated by runway length.

To achieve maximum acceleration as efficiently as possible, the body will rise at a constant rate. This postural change is a direct result of stride length and frequency gradually and smoothly increasing during each step. If there is any disruption of progressive posture, there will also be a disruptive change in stride patterns. This, of course, will affect maximum acceleration over a given distance and most likely reduce jump distance.

During the 1990 TAC Championships in Norwalk, California, Dr. James Hay, TAC/USOC biomechanist in charge of the horizontal jumps, performed a biomechanical analysis of several jumpers. One of the jumpers evaluated was future world record holder Mike Powell. The analysis determined that Powell was hav-ing difficulty with general progression of stride length.

The report of the analysis can be used to evaluate the progression and consistency of Powell's full run-up, particularly the last four strides prior to the jump. In Mike's best jump of 8.24 meters (Table 4.1), note that there is a slight difference between strides 9 and 10. There is an increase, but it is not significant. In Mike's second-best jump of 8.13 meters, stride 6 is shorter than stride 5. However, the big problem occurs in strides 18 to 23; in every trial, there is a decrease in length on nearly every stride.

Dr. Hay also evaluated Carl Lewis (see Figure 4.2 and Table 4.2). Although Lewis's evaluation only included his last four strides, in contrast to Powell's runway, you will note a general progression of stride length until the last step, which is shortened to achieve a high hip position.

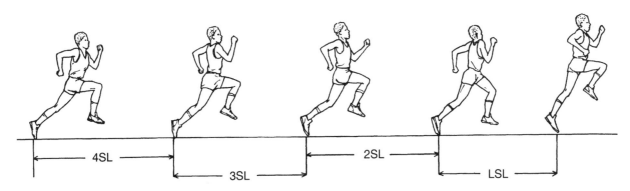

Figure 4.2   The last four strides of Carl Lewis's approach for the long jump (4SL = length of fourth to last stride; 3SL = length of third to last stride; 2SL = length of second to last stride; LSL = length of last stride).

Note. Used with permission of Dr. James Hay.

Table 4.2
Stride Lengths in Two Carl Lewis Jumps

	Trial	4SL	3SL	2SL	LSL	Distance of jump
Olympic trial, 1984	1	2.53 m (8' 3¹/₂")	2.49 m (8' 2")	2.63 m (8' 7¹/₂")	2.43 m (7' 11¹/₂")	3.71 m (28' 7")
TAC National Championship, 1987	4	2.40 m (7' 10¹/₂")	2.58 m (8' 5¹/₂")	2.86 m (9' 4¹/₂")	1.97 m (6' 5¹/₂")	8.65 m (28'4")

Note. Used with permission of Dr. James Hay.

Inconsistencies in stride length can be due to various reasons, such as wind, either behind or into the jumper, fatigue, soreness, etc. In some cases, runway length needs to be adjusted; however, most often the athlete makes the necessary adjustment subconsciously. This visual control or steering, as it is called, tends to occur so that the athlete can hit the takeoff board accurately. Some athletes are good at this; others lack this specific skill.

The coaching implication of this steering mechanism is that the automatic adjustment is completed around five steps prior to takeoff. However, the mechanical implication is that any adjustments are subtle and that velocity is not lost.

In the long jump as well as the triple jump runs, the point at which the steering seems to kick in is approximately five strides prior to takeoff. This is significant because it means that, due to the earlier adjustments, the last five strides will be the most consistent of the entire runway.

For this reason, the four-step coach's mark is established. If the athlete has determined to jump, the last four strides leading into the jump will have a constant average distance. If the average of the last four strides equals 8 feet, the coach's mark will be 32 feet from the takeoff board.

The average of the last four steps should be computed over many practice runways without the takeoff board. This is so that the athlete can accelerate through his or her entire 16 to 20 strides without having to make the steering adjustments necessary to hit the board. The coach should measure the distance from the fourth step out to the toe of the takeoff foot at foot release of the jump. This distance will provide a suitable four-step coach's mark.

As the athlete becomes stronger, new check marks must be computed. For developing athletes, this mark will progress from 6 inches to a foot within a year. Always establish the mark away from the runway, where the athlete can freewheel into the takeoff with no fear of fouling. Ideally, within reason, the coach's mark should move back gradually, depending on the athlete's ability to maintain velocity and erect posture into and off the takeoff board.

If the athlete has to reach to hit the board from the four-step mark, then due to the posture-acceleration relationship, this will cause the athlete to lean back too far and thus decelerate. Obviously, the check mark is too far from the board.

Carl Lewis

This sequence illustrates an 8.71-meter (28-foot 7-inch) jump by Carl Lewis at the 1984 Olympic length. This jump had a lower horizontal velocity than other jumps that covered greater distances.

Conversely, if the stride length begins to shorten to allow the jumper to hit the board, deceleration is again occurring and the check mark is too close to the board.

Over the years, Carl Lewis's long jumps have been evaluated in depth by Dr. Hay. In reading the various reports on Lewis, it is interesting to note that little attention was paid to his technique in the air. Most of the investigation concentrated on speed at takeoff, hip height, and stride length from the coach's mark at four strides from actual takeoff.

The distance of the coach's mark varied from 8.66 meters (28 feet 5 inches) to 10.27 meters (33 feet 8 inches). The studies indicated that Lewis's best jumps occurred when the four-stride distance was the greatest. In essence, the 33-foot 8-inch mark provided greater horizontal velocity at takeoff, resulting in a greater jump distance.

It should be noted, however, that in one competition, the 1986 TAC Meet, Lewis's fourth stride distance from takeoff was significantly longer. It increased to 10.37 meters (34 feet), and his actual long jump distances dropped to 8.16 meters (26 feet 9-1/4 inches) and 8.35 meters (27 feet 4-3/4 inches), which for Lewis were not good jumping efforts.

Transition From Run-Up to Jump

At some point, the athlete must prepare his or her body to move from a near-maximum horizontal velocity to vertical impulse. To make this transition, the jumper's hips must settle or lower. The key is to make this adjustment with as little effect on speed as possible. To accomplish this, the next to last stride must be lengthened slightly. As the stride increases a little beyond the normal acceleration length (6 feet 9 inches), the hips will lower naturally (see Tables 4.3 and 4.4). This places the hips in a position so that on the final step, the center of mass can move from a low to a high position and from initial foot contact to foot release in the jump. This is the basis of the vertical component.

Foot contact during these last two steps is also of great importance. The actual lowering during the penultimate step is enhanced by landing flat-footed with the foot directly under the hips and moving backward actively. The final step of the takeoff foot onto the board should also be flat so that the full force is directed into the board over a short time period. If the foot contact is on the toe, the ankle

trials. Although not one of his better jumps, his final four stride distances are of equal

Note. Used with permission of Dr. James Hay.

will be forced to flex, causing a dissipation of force and a longer duration on the board than desired. On the other hand, if the foot lands on the heel, it causes a braking action and a large horizontal speed reduction. The emphasis of a good takeoff is the distance (the longer, the better) the hip moves from an active foot touchdown until foot release.

Biomechanical studies of the duration of foot contact on the board have led to an interesting conclusion. Regardless of the athlete's speed coming into the board, the foot contact duration remains nearly the same. Comparing a slow athlete running at 6 meters per second (almost a jog) to an athlete running at 11 meters per second, there is almost no dif-

Table 4.3
Powell's Horizontal Velocity of Six Jumps Presented in Meters/Seconds and Distance Jumped

Trial	1	2	3	4	5	6
Distance in meters	(7.95)	(8.13)	(7.95)	(F)	(F)	(8.24)
Distance in feet	(26' 1")	26' 8$\frac{1}{4}$")	(26' 1")	(F)	(F)	(27'1$\frac{1}{2}$")
Speed in meters/seconds	(10.72)	(10.86)	(10.48)	(9.99)	(10.60)	(10.81)

Note. Data from Dr. James Hay.

Table 4.4
Comparison of Stride Length of Elite Jumper

Athlete	Fourth to last	Third to last	Second to last	Last	Distance jump
Beamon (USA)			7'10$\frac{1}{2}$"	8'6$\frac{1}{2}$"	29'2$\frac{1}{2}$"
Boston (USA)			8'3$\frac{3}{4}$"	7'10$\frac{3}{4}$"	27'2"
Ter-Ovanesyan (USSR)	7'8$\frac{1}{2}$"	7'5$\frac{1}{4}$"	8'2"	6'9"	26'10$\frac{1}{2}$"
Robertson (USA)			8'3"	6'9"	26'7$\frac{1}{4}$"
Bell (USA)			7'9$\frac{1}{2}$"	6'8$\frac{1}{4}$"	26'4$\frac{1}{2}$"
Shelby (USA)	7'5$\frac{1}{4}$"	7"$\frac{1}{2}$"	8'5$\frac{3}{4}$"	6'10$\frac{1}{4}$"	25'7$\frac{3}{4}$"
Popov (USSR)	7'7$\frac{3}{4}$"	7'4$\frac{1}{2}$"	7'10$\frac{3}{4}$"	7'1$\frac{3}{4}$"	24'11$\frac{1}{4}$"

Note. Used with permission of Dr. James Hay and the United States Olympic Committee.

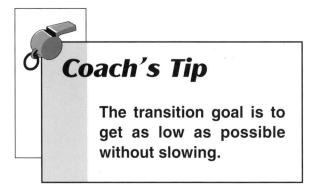

Coach's Tip

The transition goal is to get as low as possible without slowing.

ference in the duration of foot contact. With increased speed, the hips simply pass the support foot faster and produce a more effective stretch reflex in the muscles. In lay terms, the foot release speed is a desired outcome, but what actually happens is that the center of mass moves the same distance but with a lower trajectory and a much higher velocity from point A to point B.

Takeoff

The most important factor in an effective take-off is to create as large a vertical force as possible without losing horizontal speed. The actual takeoff should be thought of as the entire period from touchdown to foot release. A great deal must happen during the short time the planting foot is in contact with the board. During this time, the jumper's goal is to move the hips, or more specifically, the center of mass, from a low to as high a position as possible; at the same time, the hip height must be kept within a range that will allow speed to be maintained. Not only does the jumper want to produce as long a push as possible, he or she must also "load" the takeoff leg to initiate the myotonic stretch reflex. Physiologically, when a muscle is stretched, it then automatically contracts. The faster it is stretched, the greater the contraction. The "Plyometrics Training" section in chapter 3 describes the loading stimulus.

These two factors, coupled with transference of momentum from the leading knee and the fast-moving arms, provide the large impulse the jumper needs. At takeoff, the jumper wants as little bending or flexing of the knee

and hip as possible while going through the compression phase of the jump. As the free leg moves forward, the heel should pass close to the buttocks with the angle closed at the knee joint. This action will provide maximum speed of the knee, also expressed as angular momentum of the knee. The speed of the knee will be transferred directly into the support leg as an added force exerted into the ground. Along with a vigorous arm action, this produces a ground force that is redirected back into the jumper. As the leading knee approaches 90° from the vertical axis, the limb naturally decelerates, which, coupled with deceleration of the arms, causes an unweighting in conjunction with the extension of the ankle, knee, and hip and propels the body off the ground at precisely the same instant. In addition to the above, the jumper wants an absolute upright and extended posture to enable the center of mass to be at its ultimate height.

Long jumpers use three or four styles of takeoff. These styles vary in effectiveness and should be experimented with to see what works best.

Kick Style

This technique is used by jumpers who employ the hitch-kick jumping technique; however, it is appropriate for the jumper who anticipates the active leg cycling before a full impulse has been directed into the board. It does not allow full extension of the hips or complete application of impulse. The foot is kicked forward prior to ground release (see Figure 4.3).

Double-Arm Style

Although this style is not well known, it has been used effectively by most of the great hang-style jumpers over the past 30 years, including Robert Emmiyan and Igor Ter-Ovanesyan of the former Soviet Union and Gregory Bell of the United States. It is difficult to achieve the maximum benefits of this style without slowing the horizontal speed of the run-up; however, it is an effective way of developi

Figure 4.3 The kick-style technique.

Figure 4.4 The double-arm style.

transference of force into the takeoff leg by moving both arms in a vertical direction. For jumpers who use the hang technique, the double-arm style adapts nicely to the double-arm swing that accompanies the hang jump. Both arms move in a vertical direction to produce high hip height and a large impulse (see Figure 4.4).

Sprint Takeoff

This style has a classical single-arm action that resembles a sprinter in full stride (see Figure 4.5). It is preferred by most coaches and is often emphasized by technical writers who are attempting to describe a takeoff that conserves speed while running off the board. This technique can be adapted to any style of jump but is best used with the hitch kick. Although this style is the most popular, it is not necessarily the best. It does not provide maximum arm impulse into the takeoff leg and often does not allow the body to be upright and extended. However, it does provide a high hip position.

Power Sprint or Bounding Takeoff

If the primary goal is to provide maximum impulse along with speed through the takeoff

and a high hip position, the bounding takeoff is probably the best choice for the hitch-kick jumper. It would rank slightly ahead of the double-arm style because it allows for speed maintenance into the takeoff. As shown in Figure 4.6, the right arm is extended, which at takeoff provides some counterrotation to the forward rotation that occurs while the athlete is airborne. Because of the right arm extension, the bounding takeoff blends nicely into the flight behavior of both the hitch-kick and hang styles.

Airborne Technique

As discussed previously, the flight curve of the long jumper is determined solely at takeoff and is the result of velocity and takeoff angle. This curve cannot be altered by any motions performed by the long jumper during the flight phase of the jump.

Theoretically, the distance attained by the jumper would be determined by the speed and angle achieved at takeoff. However, the human body reacts differently than a projectile shot out of a cannon (see Figure 1.4, p. 8).

When the jumping foot is planted, a biomechanical phenomenon called *forward rotation*

Figure 4.5 The sprint takeoff.

Figure 4.6 The power sprint or bounding takeoff.

occurs. During foot contact, deceleration or blocking of forward speed takes place. The amount of this deceleration depends on two factors: the distance forward of the hips at which the foot strikes or the rearward speed of the foot and leg prior to foot strike. When braking occurs, the original speed is transferred upward; therefore, all parts of the body above the foot begin to accelerate beyond the stationary foot.

In most track and field events, this "hinge moment" or blocking is utilized to produce optimum performances, especially in the throws. However, in the long jump and triple jump, the added speed of the upper body causes an undesirable forward rotation (see Figure 4.7). If the action is unchecked, the body goes into a frontal somersault motion about the hips, causing the feet to land in the pit prematurely or, even worse, a face-first landing.

In jumping events, especially while moving at high speeds, the foot contacts the ground at a point in front of the center of mass. The

Figure 4.7 In-flight forward body rotation during the long jump.

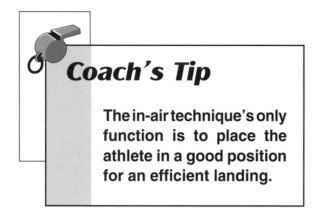

Coach's Tip

The in-air technique's only function is to place the athlete in a good position for an efficient landing.

distance in front of the hips is determined by the amount of vertical velocity needed. The body pivots over and past the takeoff foot, causing a rotation around the transverse axis through the foot. Rotation is also about a transverse axis through the center of mass.

This action carries on into the flight path of the jumper and creates an undesirable forward rotation in the long jump. The jumper creates body manipulations that either reduce or eliminate this problem during the flight phase of the jump (Doolittle, 1988).

Considering the above discussion, the only reason for any in-flight activity is to prevent or reduce this natural forward rotation. Such activity will not cause the hips to travel any additional distance; however, it will provide better balance and place the body in a position for a more efficient landing.

There are basically three styles of in-air activity for the long jumper: the sail, the hang, and some version of the hitch kick. All others are adaptations of these three styles. Only two of these styles are effective when judged according to biomechanical principles.

Sail Technique

The sail technique is the simplest because it involves no complex movement; however, it is seldom used by successful jumpers because of the difficulty in keeping the body balanced through the entire parabola of the flight pattern. The jumper is likely to begin a premature rotation, and the weight in front of the hips adds impetus to this already problematic forward rotation. The free leg moves directly out in front of the hips and is soon joined by the takeoff leg. This large amount of total weight moves the center of gravity out in front of the hips, and the jumper's legs quickly drop into the pit before the flight curve is completed (see Figure 4.8).

Hang Style

Although this style has been in mothballs for about 20 years, it has recently received much attention due to the efforts of Robert Emmiyan of the former Soviet Union. This has caused a resurgence of the hang-style jump.

After the takeoff, the jumper allows the free leg to drop until it is directly under the hips (see Figure 4.9). This long, narrow silhouette of the body causes the least possible rotation as both the arm and leg (hand and foot) are a maximum distance away from the hips (the theoretical center of mass). As we learned in chapter 1, long levers rotate more slowly than short levers.

The free leg, which has dropped directly under the hips, will eventually be joined by the takeoff leg. We call this position 180°. At this point, the knees of both legs are directly under

Figure 4.8 The sail technique.

Figure 4.9   The hang style.

the hips. This is the most stable in-flight position because very little rotation can occur. The 180° leg position is held for a brief period and then reduced to 90° as the legs flex at the knees. It is important that the knees be flexed so that the feet swing through to land with the fastest possible angular momentum.

The arms are extended at the elbow and brought around to reach high above the head parallel to the 90° position of the knees. This flexed angle allows the legs to recover to the front quickly, similar to the recovery leg of a sprinter.

The "old style" of the hang (shown in Figure 4.10), which is characterized by an arched back, probably should not be taught because it decreases the length of the lever formed in the 90° knee bend.

Hitch-Kick Style

The hitch kick is described as a continual running action during the flight phase of the jump (see Figure 4.11). Over the years, this style has produced the best marks by the top jumpers in the world. Again, the only purpose of this cycling motion is to counteract and reduce forward rotation during the jump. This style is designed to set up secondary rotations of both the arms and legs that mechanically counteract the rotations established at takeoff.

A variety of hitch-kick styles is prevalent among long jumpers at all levels of skill development. The biggest difference is probably found between the elite athlete and the young jumper who cannot yet achieve the time in the air required for a full two-and-one-half-step hitch-kick jump.

The majority of athletes who employ this style of jump should use a single-step arm and leg cycle. Although less popular, this style is more suitable for the young jumper because

Figure 4.10   The outdated hang style, characterized by an arched back.

Figure 4.11   The hitch-kick style.

Landing

the full two-and-one-half step technique usually causes a premature landing. For those who cannot achieve the full two and one-half steps, it is probably best to work with the hang style of jump rather than combat the potential of a premature landing.

The effectiveness of this style is evaluated based on the body's posture in the air after takeoff. Problems with using the hitch kick are most likely to occur when the athlete attempts to begin the cycling motions prior to taking full advantage of the takeoff impulse. The jumper must execute the full takeoff (i.e., moving the hips as high and as far forward of the board as anatomically possible) before beginning any in-flight maneuvers. Figure 4.12 shows trunk, head, and arm position at landing and the height of the center of mass in a variety of positions. Point (a) provides the lowest possible position of center of gravity, thereby denoting the jumper who was best able to remain on the flight curve for the longest possible time.

The main objective of the landing is to allow the flight curve to be fully utilized. To attain this goal, the jumper must accomplish two components. The first is to position the feet at a maximum horizontal distance in front of the hips; however, this motion can be overemphasized because complete utilization of this principle will inevitably cause the jumper to fall back at landing (see Figure 4.13). The second component is to allow the hips or center of gravity to sink to the lowest possible position at ground contact. This is best achieved just prior to landing if the feet are aligned slightly above the normal parabolic curve of the center of mass. Therefore, prior to landing, the jumper wants his or her feet to be higher than the hips.

Compared to the other jumping events, the long jump is relatively simple. In this country, from the high school level up, with the huge talent pool of speed, it would be wise to begin

Figure 4.12   Trunk, head, and arm position at a variety of landings. The solid circle denotes the center of mass in each position. The landing shown in (a) is the most efficient because the center of mass is in the lowest possible position.

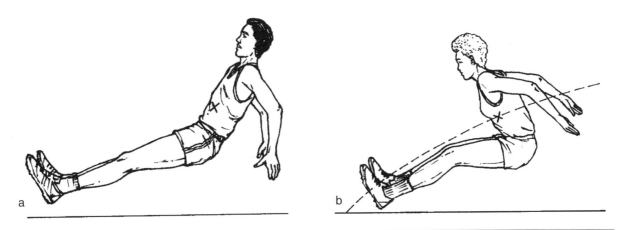

Figure 4.13   Landing technique: (a) incorrect fallback; (b) correct landing.

generating the same enthusiasm for the long jump as we do for the sprints. Not all long jumpers can become great sprinters—but certainly most great sprinters have the potential of becoming great long jumpers.

Long Jump Training Program

Workout samples for the long jump follow for your review (see Figures 4.14 to 4.17). There is a sample weekly workout for the general preparation, specific preparation, power develop-

ment, and competition mesocycles. Keep in mind that these are only samples. Although they are appropriate for a college-level athlete, they should not be used as is. Workouts should be designed to fit a specific athlete and can only be developed with complete understanding of his or her capabilities, including lead-up activities, experience, and talent level.

General training fundamentals are listed in the left column of each workout. The specific activities for each day of the week are listed in the right column. Each weekly workout includes running, and emphasis is placed on strength, technical, multithrow, flexibility, coordination, and psychological areas.

General Preparation Workout

1. **Easy jogging**
2. **Warm-up drills:**
   - (a) High leg to 50
   - (b) Fast legs to 50
   - (c) Cariokas
   - (d) A-B-Cs to 50
   - (e) Stretching
3. **Skipping:**
   - (a) Standard
   - (b) Power
   - (c) Double arms
4. **Stadium stairs:**
   - (a) Sprinting up
   - (b) Springing down
   - (c) Hopping up
     - (1) Single leg
     - (2) Double legs
   - (d) Hopping down
     - (1) Single leg
     - (2) Double legs
5. **Power runs:**
   - (a) Hills
   - (b) Belts
6. **Downhills:**
   - (a) General
   - (b) With takeoff
7. **Speed bounding:**
   - (a) Single leg
   - (b) Double legs
   - (c) RR-LL
   - (d) H-S-S-S-H
   - (e) From 8 steps
8. **Power bounding:**
   - (a) Single leg
   - (b) Double legs
   - (c) RR-LL
9. **Landing drills:**
   - (a) Split
   - (b) Alternate
   - (c) Standing on knees
   - (d) Full
10. **Penultimate step drills:**
    - (a) 8 steps
    - (b) 4 steps
11. **Hurdle hops:**
    - (a) Flat
    - (b) Box to 5 hurdles
    - (c) Box to 8 hurdles
12. **Coach's mark to takeoff timing**
13. **Simulated runway:**
    - (a) Full
    - (b) 8 steps
    - (c) 6 steps
14. **Weights:**
    - (a) Special
      - (1) Clean & jerk
      - (2) Single-leg squats
      - (3) Weighted vest
      - (4) Lunges
    - (b) Circuit
    - (c) Power strength (general)
    - (d) Arm drills
15. **Running sets:**
    - (a) 40
    - (b) 50
    - (c) 60
    - (d) 70
    - (e) 80
    - (f) 100
    - (g) 110
    - (h) 150
    - (i) 180
    - (j) 200
    - (k) 300
    - (l) 322
    - (m) 400
    - (n) 500
    - (o) 550
    - (p) 600
    - (q) 800
    - (r) 1,000
16. **Hurdles:** (same as above)
17. **Timed drop-downs:**
    - (a) 20-30-20
    - (b) 20-40-20
    - (c) 20-50-20
    - (d) 20-60

(continued)

Figure 4.14   Sample long jump workout during the general preparation mesocycle.

18. **Running drills:**
    (a) Backward
    (b) Circle
    (c) Figure 8
    (d) Side hills
    (e) Pop-ups

19. **Boxes:**
    (a) 14-16' bounding R-L-R-L;
        16-18' bounding R-L-R-L
    (b) RR-LL
    (c) Single leg through both legs
    (d) **HJ drills**
        (1) Table jumping
        (2) Ground-to-box-to-ground jumping
        (3) Ground-to-low-box jumping
    (e) **LJ drills**
        (1) Ground-to-box-to-ground jumping
        (2) Ground-to-low-box jumping

20. Meet with coach

21. **Films:**
    (a) Study session
    (b) To be filmed

22. Rehabilitation

23. Precompetition warm-up/check marks

24. Pool

25. **Medicine ball series:**
    (a) Double arms
    (b) Abdominal

26. Running circuit

27. Distance run

Legend of Work-to-Rest Ratios

Monday

(1 to 1 mi) (stretch) (2 a-b-c-d × 6 to 50)
(3b × 4 to 80) (8a-b × 6 to 30)
(9d measured from 8 steps)
(15k × 1) (15j × 1) (15h × 1) (15f × 2)
(cooldown)

Tuesday

(1 to 2 mi) (stretch) (2 a-b-c-d × 6 to 40)
(7a-b to 100 from 6 steps × 3)
(14 special power program)
(cooldown with swim)

Wednesday

(1 to 4 mi)
(5a × 4 to 150 drop-downs)
(1 to 1-1/2 mi)

Thursday

(1 to 1 mi) (stretch) (a-b-c-d × 4 to 40)
(13a full—establish marks)
(15h × 4)
(14 easy day on power program)

Friday

Basketball—wear proper shoes

Saturday

Rest

Sunday

(14 2nd session of power program)

Figure 4.14   *(continued)*

General Preparation Workout

1. **Easy jogging**
2. **Warm-up drills:**
   - (a) High leg to 50
   - (b) Fast legs to 50
   - (c) Cariokas
   - (d) A-B-Cs to 50
   - (e) Stretching
3. **Skipping:**
   - (a) Standard
   - (b) Power
   - (c) Double arms
4. **Stadium stairs:**
   - (a) Sprinting up
   - (b) Springing down
   - (c) Hopping up
     - (1) Single leg
     - (2) Double legs
   - (d) Hopping down
     - (1) Single leg
     - (2) Double legs
5. **Power runs:**
   - (a) Hills
   - (b) Belts
6. **Downhills:**
   - (a) General
   - (b) With takeoff
7. **Speed bounding:**
   - (a) Single leg
   - (b) Double legs
   - (c) RR-LL
   - (d) H-S-S-S-H
   - (e) From 8 steps
8. **Power bounding:**
   - (a) Single leg
   - (b) Double legs
   - (c) RR-LL
9. **Landing drills:**
   - (a) Split
   - (b) Alternate
   - (c) Standing on knees
   - (d) Full
10. **Penultimate step drills:**
    - (a) 8 steps
    - (b) 4 steps
11. **Hurdle hops:**
    - (a) Flat
    - (b) Box to 5 hurdles
    - (c) Box to 8 hurdles
12. **Coach's mark to takeoff timing**
13. **Simulated runway:**
    - (a) Full
    - (b) 8 steps
    - (c) 6 steps
14. **Weights:**
    - (a) Special
      - (1) Clean & jerk
      - (2) Single-leg squats
      - (3) Weighted vest
      - (4) Lunges
    - (b) Circuit
    - (c) Power strength (general)
    - (d) Arm drills
15. **Running sets:**
    - (a) 40
    - (b) 50
    - (c) 60
    - (d) 70
    - (e) 80
    - (f) 100
    - (g) 110
    - (h) 150
    - (i) 180
    - (j) 200
    - (k) 300
    - (l) 322
    - (m) 400
    - (n) 500
    - (o) 550
    - (p) 600
    - (q) 800
    - (r) 1,000
16. **Hurdles:** (same as above)
17. **Timed drop-downs:**
    - (a) 20-30-20
    - (b) 20-40-20
    - (c) 20-50-20
    - (d) 20-60

(continued)

Figure 4.15 Sample long jump workout during the specific preparation mesocycle.

18. **Running drills:**
    (a) Backward
    (b) Circle
    (c) Figure 8
    (d) Side hills
    (e) Pop-ups

19. **Boxes:**
    (a) 14-16' bounding R-L-R-L;
        16-18' bounding R-L-R-L
    (b) RR-LL
    (c) Single leg through both legs
    (d) **HJ drills**
        (1) Table jumping
        (2) Ground-to-box-to-ground jumping
        (3) Ground-to-low-box jumping
    (e) **LJ drills**
        (1) Ground-to-box-to-ground jumping
        (2) Ground-to-low-box jumping

20. Meet with coach

21 **Films:**
    (a) Study session
    (b) To be filmed

22. Rehabilitation

23. Precompetition warm-up/check marks

24. Pool

25. **Medicine ball series:**
    (a) Double arms
    (b) Abdominal

26. Running circuit

27. Distance run

Legend of Work-to-Rest Ratios

Monday

(1 to 3 mi) (2 a-b-c-d × 6 ea.)
(2e) (5a × 8 gradual drop-down)
(1 to 1 mi)

Tuesday

(1 to 2 mi) (2 a-b-c-d × 4 ea.)
(8a × 4 to 60) (8b × 6 to 60)
(18a × 6 to 40)
(14 posted work)

Wednesday

(1 to 2 mi) (2 a-b-c-d × 5 ea.)
(4a × 2 steady) (15e × steady)
(4a × 3 steady) (21 - 9a-b × 8)
(21 of 8 a&b × 4 to 14 ground contact)
(cooldown jogging)

Thursday

(21 review with coach) (early meeting)
(1 to 1 mi) (2 a-b-c-d × 6 ea. to 40)
(18h to 90% × 6)
(14 full posted workout)

Friday

Rest or special activity

Saturday

Rest

Sunday

(14 full posted session)

Figure 4.15 *(continued)*

Power Development Workout

1. **Easy jogging**
2. **Warm-up drills:**
   (a) High leg to 50
   (b) Fast legs to 50
   (c) Cariokas
   (d) A-B-Cs to 50
   (e) Stretching
3. **Skipping:**
   (a) Standard
   (b) Power
   (c) Double arms
4. **Stadium stairs:**
   (a) Sprinting up
   (b) Springing down
   (c) Hopping up
       (1) Single leg
       (2) Double legs
   (d) Hopping down
       (1) Single leg
       (2) Double legs
5. **Power runs:**
   (a) Hills
   (b) Belts
6. **Downhills:**
   (a) General
   (b) With takeoff
7. **Speed bounding:**
   (a) Single leg
   (b) Double legs
   (c) RR-LL
   (d) H-S-S-S-H
   (e) From 8 steps
8. **Power bounding:**
   (a) Single leg
   (b) Double legs
   (c) RR-LL
9. **Landing drills:**
   (a) Split
   (b) Alternate
   (c) Standing on knees
   (d) Full
10. **Penultimate step drills:**
    (a) 8 steps
    (b) 4 steps
11. **Hurdle hops:**
    (a) Flat
    (b) Box to 5 hurdles
    (c) Box to 8 hurdles
12. **Coach's mark to takeoff timing**
13. **Simulated runway:**
    (a) Full
    (b) 8 steps
    (c) 6 steps
14. **Weights:**
    (a) Special
        (1) Clean & jerk
        (2) Single-leg squats
        (3) Weighted vest
        (4) Lunges
    (b) Circuit
    (c) Power strength (general)
    (d) Arm drills
15. **Running sets:**
    (a) 40
    (b) 50
    (c) 60
    (d) 70
    (e) 80
    (f) 100
    (g) 110
    (h) 150
    (i) 180
    (j) 200
    (k) 300
    (l) 322
    (m) 400
    (n) 500
    (o) 550
    (p) 600
    (q) 800
    (r) 1,000
16. **Hurdles:** (same as above)
17. **Timed drop-downs:**
    (a) 20-30-20
    (b) 20-40-20
    (c) 20-50-20
    (d) 20-60

(continued)

Figure 4.16   Sample long jump workout during the power development mesocycle.

18. **Running drills:**
    (a) Backward
    (b) Circle
    (c) Figure 8
    (d) Side hills
    (e) Pop-ups

19. **Boxes:**
    (a) 14-16' bounding R-L-R-L;
        16-18' bounding R-L-R-L
    (b) RR-LL
    (c) Single leg through both legs
    (d) **HJ drills**
        (1) Table jumping
        (2) Ground-to-box-to-ground jumping
        (3) Ground-to-low-box jumping
    (e) **LJ drills**
        (1) Ground-to-box-to-ground jumping
        (2) Ground-to-low-box jumping

20. Meet with coach

21 **Films:**
    (a) Study session
    (b) To be filmed

22. Rehabilitation

23. Precompetition warm-up/check marks

24. Pool

25. **Medicine ball series:**
    (a) Double arms
    (b) Abdominal

26. Running circuit

27. Distance run

Legend of
Work-to-Rest Ratios

Monday

(1 to 2 mi) (stretch) (2a-b-c-d to 40)
(13 a × 4) (15h × 4 drop-downs)
(3b to 16 ground contacts)

Tuesday

(1 to 800) (stretch) (2a-b-c-d to 30 × 5 ea.)
(14 power 1/2 squats—1/2 squats—single-leg
bounds × 14 ground contacts) (inverted-leg press)
(8 × stair single-leg hops) power clean –
power clean – box-to-hurdle jumps × 8 snatches

Wednesday

(1 to 800) (stretch) (2a-b-c-d to 50 × 4)
(17d not timed × 6)
(cooldown)

Thursday

(1 to 800) (stretch) (2a-b-c-d to 40 × 5 ea.)
(15g × 4 – 15k × 1)
(14 power cycle – Day 2)
(cooldown)

Friday

(1 to 1 mi) (stretch)
(power hill runs to 150 × 5 drop-downs)
(3b × 5)

Saturday

Rest

Sunday

(1 to 800) (stretch)
(14 power cycle – Day 3 – repeat of Tuesday)

Figure 4.16   (*continued*)

Competition Workout

1. **Easy jogging**
2. **Warm-up drills:**
   - (a) High leg to 50
   - (b) Fast legs to 50
   - (c) Cariokas
   - (d) A-B-Cs to 50
   - (e) Stretching
3. **Skipping:**
   - (a) Standard
   - (b) Power
   - (c) Double arms
4. **Stadium stairs:**
   - (a) Sprinting up
   - (b) Springing down
   - (c) Hopping up
     - (1) Single leg
     - (2) Double legs
   - (d) Hopping down
     - (1) Single leg
     - (2) Double legs
5. **Power runs:**
   - (a) Hills
   - (b) Belts
6. **Downhills:**
   - (a) General
   - (b) With takeoff
7. **Speed bounding:**
   - (a) Single leg
   - (b) Double legs
   - (c) RR-LL
   - (d) H-S-S-S-H
   - (e) From 8 steps
8. **Power bounding:**
   - (a) Single leg
   - (b) Double legs
   - (c) RR-LL
9. **Landing drills:**
   - (a) Split
   - (b) Alternate
   - (c) Standing on knees
   - (d) Full
10. **Penultimate step drills:**
    - (a) 8 steps
    - (b) 4 steps

11. **Hurdle hops:**
    - (a) Flat
    - (b) Box to 5 hurdles
    - (c) Box to 8 hurdles
12. Coach's mark to takeoff timing
13. **Simulated runway:**
    - (a) Full
    - (b) 8 steps
    - (c) 6 steps
14. **Weights:**
    - (a) Special
      - (1) Clean & jerk
      - (2) Single-leg squats
      - (3) Weighted vest
      - (4) Lunges
    - (b) Circuit
    - (c) Power strength (general)
    - (d) Arm drills
15. **Running sets:**
    - (a) 40
    - (b) 50
    - (c) 60
    - (d) 70
    - (e) 80
    - (f) 100
    - (g) 110
    - (h) 150
    - (i) 180
    - (j) 200
    - (k) 300
    - (l) 322
    - (m) 400
    - (n) 500
    - (o) 550
    - (p) 600
    - (q) 800
    - (r) 1,000
16. **Hurdles:** (same as above)
17. **Timed drop-downs:**
    - (a) 20-30-20
    - (b) 20-40-20
    - (c) 20-50-20
    - (d) 20-60

(continued)

Figure 4.17   Sample long jump workout during the competition mesocycle.

18. **Running drills:**
    (a) Backward
    (b) Circle
    (c) Figure 8
    (d) Side hills
    (e) Pop-ups

19. **Boxes:**
    (a) 14-16' bounding R-L-R-L;
        16-18' bounding R-L-R-L
    (b) RR-LL
    (c) Single leg through both legs
    (d) **HJ drills**
        (1) Table jumping
        (2) Ground-to-box-to-ground jumping
        (3) Ground-to-low-box jumping
    (e) **LJ drills**
        (1) Ground-to-box-to-ground jumping
        (2) Ground-to-low-box jumping

20. Meet with coach

21 **Films:**
    (a) Study session
    (b) To be filmed

22. Rehabilitation

23. Precompetition warm-up/check marks

24. Pool

25. **Medicine ball series:**
    (a) Double arms
    (b) Abdominal

26. Running circuit

27. Distance run

Legend of
Work-to-Rest Ratios

Monday

(1 to 1 mi) (stretch) (2 a-b-c-d × 5 to 40)
(17a × 5 drop-downs)
(7a × 40 to 12 ground contacts)
(15b × 4)
(8 ladder drills for acceleration and tempo)

Tuesday

(1 to 1 mi) (stretch) (2 a-b-c-d × 4)
(7d × 4 to 80) (13a full) (4a × 3 drop-downs)
(14 competition cycle)

Wednesday

(1 to 2 mi) (stretch) (2 a-b-c-d × 4)
(17b × 4 all timed for drop-down)
(15e × 4 drop-downs)
(9 a-b-d × 4 ea.)
(8 ladder drills)

Thursday

(1 to 800) (stretch) (2 a-b-c-d × 4)
(4a × 3 for time—best of year)
(6a with takeoff × 8)
(14 competition cycle)

Friday

(full warm-up at site of competition)
(3 × full runway check)

Saturday

Competition

Sunday

(14 full competition cycle—last lifting session
until after conference competition); those
traveling to NCAA will lift 5 more times

Figure 4.17   *(continued)*

Chapter 5
Triple Jump

The triple jump is the only one of the jumping events that does not require a big explosive effort. This jump is actually a continuous sequence of movements, with each phase dependent on the preceding activity. Although each segment can be isolated, it is important to keep the total activity in mind.

In the triple jump, more than any other event, it is essential to distinguish symptoms from causes. It is useless to concentrate your energies on analyzing the step phase without going back to the hop phase, and especially to how the landing occurred at the end of the hop—for the hop phase dictates almost totally what can and cannot occur in the step phase and later in the jump phase.

Keys to Triple Jumping

- Maintain high speed during all three takeoffs while applying impulse with the arms

- Achieve maximum height of the hips at takeoff in each phase

- Achieve a low hip angle at takeoff in each phase

- Maintain an upright body position and balance in flight

- Achieve an efficient landing by keeping the hips on the predetermined flight curve as long as possible during the jump phase

As with other jumping events, the height of the hip into the hop and then into each succeeding jump will create efficiency of distance during each phase. The higher the hips, the greater the flight curve.

The angle of the hips going into each flight phase must be as low as possible. As the jumper's speed begins to diminish through each phase, the takeoff angle will automatically begin to increase through the step and jump phases. Elite triple jumpers will average under 14° for the hop and step and then move up to a little under 22° for the jump phase.

Balance and rotations are always a product of forward rotation at the takeoff of each jump phase. Here angular momentum is in a frontal or horizontal direction. Lateral rotations are generally caused by an uneven arm thrust or by landing with inappropriate foot support or placement.

Finally, an efficient landing is achieved by keeping the hips on the flight curve as long as possible. Good landings are a product of the takeoff from the step phase. The objective is to reduce forward rotation as much as possible.

Speed Conversion

In an attempt to gain maximum distances from the hop and the step, an athlete may make ground contact with the foot well ahead of the hips, causing an undesirable braking action. To minimize the braking effect, the jumper must make ground contact just ahead of the center of mass (hips). To do this, the jumper must be patient, waiting for the ground to come up to the foot rather than reaching for the ground. The athlete should not rush the extension of the knee and hip.

The grounding foot must be very active. This foot should move backward as rapidly as possible in a short pawing motion. Foot contact with the ground should be minimized, meaning the jumper must get onto and off the ground in the shortest possible time. The best way to ensure this is to think of the hop and the step as takeoffs rather than as landings.

A good jumper is able to transfer large amounts of force or impulse into the ground.

When generating forces from the ground in the three phases of the triple jump, there are two objectives. One is loading of the stretch reflexes of the muscle, specifically the quadriceps of the supporting leg. The other is the transfer of forces from the free-swinging knee and arms. When a contracted muscle is forced to stretch, the result is a "supercontraction." When this stretching is forced into a shorter time duration, muscle contractability is magnified. For this reason, the jumper must develop the ability to place the leg in a position that provides a loading effect and, more important, to have a ground contact of very short duration. This is achieved with a flat-footed landing just ahead of the hips.

Coach's Tip

Good triple jumping means developing maximum speed in the run, then maintaining as much momentum as possible until landing.

The swinging actions of the free leg and the arms are important sources of impulse at each takeoff. A powerful swinging motion of the free leg is necessary. The leg should be brought through flexed at the knee to provide maximum angular momentum. To time the arm movements with the strike of the knee, the arms should be moved through the largest possible range of motion and kept out away from the body. This aids in lateral balance. The greater the speed of the leg and the greater the range of motion in the arms, the greater the force generated into the ground.

Arm and leg positions just prior to ground contact with the support leg are important to initiate a significant transference of force into the compression-loading leg. Figures 5.1 and

Figure 5.1   Arm and leg position in the double-arm technique.

Figure 5.2   Arm and leg position in the single-arm technique.

5.2 show arm and leg positions before ground contact. These examples show both the double-arm and single-arm styles.

Posture is important throughout each of the three phases because all of the forces generated must move through the hips and not the shoulders. The body should be kept tall and erect. This is especially important to ensure that the grounding foot lands under the hips. An additional factor to recognize is that the arm opposite the free leg will have the greater range of motion. Regardless of whether the double- or single-arm style is used, the motion of this opposite arm should be emphasized.

Double-Arm Versus Single-Arm Styles

Several triple jump styles have evolved over the years. The primary difference in these styles is the arm action used—single, double, or a combination of both. It is best to adopt the style most suited to the individual athlete's abilities.

In the 1960s, the leading triple jumper was Josef Schmidt, who used a single-arm style. For his era, he exhibited very good speed at around 10.5 seconds for the 100 meters. Because of this, he made momentum a priority and labeled his technique "the flat method," indicating a low or flat first phase in the hop. During his development stages, he actively sought to reduce his first phase distance from around 21 feet to a little more than 19 feet. His distance ratio was 35% on the hop, 30% on the step, and 35% on the jump over a total distance of 55 feet 10 inches.

Schmidt used this flat method because he felt a low hop would enable him to position his support foot more directly under his hips and thus maintain speed throughout the first phase. As discussed earlier, this is a valid theory. Up to that time, triple jumpers did not use a double-arm action for any phase of the jump. Foot placement was considered the best way to conserve speed, and the main concern was to maintain enough speed to get through the three phases. For this reason, many early jumpers had a comparatively short step phase.

The next style to emerge in this evolutionary progression was the classic Soviet style called the "Soviet Double Arm." This technique, identified especially with Viktor Saneyev, who jumped 57 feet 2 inches, used a double-arm takeoff on all three phases of the jump. Saneyev's technique was characterized by relatively high hop and step phases followed by a flat jump phase.

Certainly this method has some merits, especially the ability to maximize the use of both arms in applying force. Strength seemed to be the main ingredient for the Soviet jumpers. The style allowed better balance than the earlier single-arm technique, and to a large extent, it prevented much of the unwanted forward rotation. The reason for this was a steep descent off the hop and step, allowing easy foot placement under the hips. For most athletes, using the double-arm style would increase ground contact duration. However, the real problem with the Soviet style was the inability to maintain speed from the last two running strides into the takeoff due to the difficulty of getting both arms in position for takeoff. For the novice and not so strong jumper, the double-arm style represents real problems with both speed and strength.

Following Saneyev, the U.S. jumpers came into the picture, exemplified by Willie Banks and Michael Conley, both of whom were superb athletes. At first, the U.S. system followed the Soviets in using the double-arm style, but eventually U.S. athletes gradually converted to a single-arm hop, a double-arm step, and a double-arm jump.

In comparing the percentage of jump ratios for U.S. athletes to those described for Schmidt, Conley's ratio is 34-31.5-34.5 and Banks's is 35-31-34 (Susanka, 1987). These figures closely resemble Schmidt's with his so-called flat, speed-oriented style.

Next, Khristo Markov of Bulgaria rose to prominence using another modified jumping technique. He used a very powerful, straight single-arm thrust into the hop and step, terminating the jump with a double arm. Although it looks unorthodox and laterally unbalanced, he jumped 57 feet 9-1/2 inches for an Olympic record. Analyzed during the World Championship competition, Markov's ratio percentages were 36-30-34.

Three Phases of Triple Jumping

As pointed out at the beginning of the chapter, it is not a good idea to view the parts or phases of the triple jumping event as separate entities. Remember that problems in one sequence can always be traced back to a preceding sequence. This concept should be kept in mind while reading the following discussion of the various phases of the triple jump.

Phase 1: The Hop

For the long jump, we stated that the horizontal component is twice as important as the vertical component. For the triple jump, the horizontal

Coach's Tip

In dealing with specific problems that occur in any phase of the triple jump, the solution will be found in the preceding phase of the jump. For example, difficulty in the step is caused by improper technique in the hop phase.

speed component ratio is 3:1. Thus, good triple jump performance requires a very low takeoff angle and very high running speed. The angle must be well under 16° for an effective jump. In the triple jump, there is little need for a complicated transition from speed to lift. The planting foot is more directly under the hips than in all of the other jumping events.

The definition of the word *hop* implies certain tendencies that describe the mechanics of this phase. As the jumper takes off from the ground on a designated leg, the movement induces a backward recovery of the same leg. It then swings forward a second time, so that the jumper lands on the same foot. After ground release of the takeoff foot, the jumping leg is flexed at the knee, and the hip pulls the leg through to a nearly 90° angle in front of the body. After reaching this position, the leg is hitch kicked back behind the body and flexed at the knee with the heel up near the hips. From here, the knee begins to recover to the front again. When the leg is forward of the hips, it is partially extended and can move with great range of motion and momentum back down to the ground. Prior to grounding and throughout the support phase, the leg must remain active. The foot lands just forward of the hips, settling into a flat position. The heel lands first but with no braking effect. The foot quickly rolls to a fully flat position and then up onto the ball, an action resembling a rocking-chair motion.

In deciding which leg is preferable for the hop, experience usually indicates that the stronger of the two provides the most efficiency. The hopping leg will soon become the step leg, which means the strong leg will be used for two of the three jumps. More important, the strong leg will be used during times when the horizontal speed is greatest, thus providing the best means of support, loading, and takeoff during the hop and step phases.

In preparing for the hop, one of the most important aspects of the jump is the speed and frequency of leg turnover, along with an upright and tall posture. The acceleration progression described in chapter 2 should be established so that horizontal speed is at maximum at least two strides prior to takeoff. This means that, due to complete acceleration, the body will naturally be upright. In addition, the foot strike is directly under the hips. The jumper desires maximum leg turnover speed. To allow an *active forward run off* the board for the low-angled hop, the last two transition steps, although not as pronounced as in other jumping events, would still be "flat-flat." The first of the two foot placements, or the penultimate step, is allowed to flatten so that the ankle, knee, and hips are slightly flexed. This lowers the center of mass without adversely affecting running speed. The takeoff step is also flat and grounded just slightly ahead of the hips. The purpose of the fully flat takeoff foot is to load up the quadriceps and calf muscles to provide the supercontraction and to minimize ground contact duration. The compressing leg should never be allowed to flex or bend more than 120°-140° (knee position). If the takeoff foot lands on either the toe or the heel, it will dissipate a lot of ground force, which is necessary for a good speed-maintaining hop. In addition, a heel landing causes a braking of horizontal momentum and a backward lean, which, in addition to slowing the athlete, tends to cause him or her to back away from the running takeoff.

The active forward run off the board is necessary to maintain horizontal speed. The head and chest should remain tall and upright and should never be directed upward or backward

Coach's Tip

The two primary enhancements to an effective hop, step, and jump are not allowing the landing foot to strike the ground too far in front of the hips and keeping the landing foot *actively* moving backward.

ing and lengthening the position of the trunk, arms, and legs (see Figure 5.3). Lengthening the arms and legs places them in a position to generate maximum transference of force into the foot strike and takeoff.

The arm action of the hop is a matter of choice, as explained earlier in this chapter. The single-arm style is preferable for the majority of jumpers because of the ease with which it is

during either the penultimate or takeoff strides. Throughout the hop phase and beyond, the eyes should focus on a level horizontal point. This encourages an upright posture and helps maintain speed. At takeoff, the knee of the free leg should move up and forward. The emphasis here is again on the horizontal rather than the vertical.

During the flight phase, the jumper employs the mechanics of minimizing and slowing forward rotation. This is accomplished by extend-

Figure 5.3   Minimizing and slowing forward rotation by extending the position of the trunk, arms, and legs.

Willie Banks

This is a wire form analysis of Willie Banks's 17.6-meter (57-foot 9-inch) triple jump at the 1987 11-1/2-inch) world record jump, the length of the hop phase (see Table 5.1) in this jump has decrease in his horizontal velocity going into the hop. Increasing the distance of the hop phase

performed and the jumper's ability to maintain horizontal speed through transition and take-off (see Figures 5.1 and 5.2). If using the double-arm style, the jumper should never allow both arms to move behind the body at the same time when moving into the hop. Instead, the arm opposite the jumping leg should be delayed at the hip and then timed to move forward with the other arm as the takeoff foot hits the board.

Regardless of whether a single- or double-arm action is used, the emphasis should be on forward motion rather than vertical. Vertical forces occurring at this time would cause a reduction of speed on landing. The parabola for the hop should be low going up and consequently low coming down. The angle of takeoff is determined by arm action, foot placement, and body posture.

Phase 2: The Step

· Without question, the second phase of the triple jump is the most troublesome and difficult to maneuver and the most difficult to integrate into the overall jump. It is a combination of a supported landing and then a jump, with the athlete moving from one foot at takeoff to a landing on the opposite foot.

There are no major differences between the objectives for this phase and those outlined for

Table 5.1
Comparison of Length of Hop Phase

Athlete/meet	Minimum	Average	Maximum
Harrison (1988)	6.63 (21'9")	6.76 (22'2$\frac{1}{4}$")	6.88 (22'7")
Harrison (1986)	6.01 (19'8$\frac{3}{4}$")	6.59 (21' 7$\frac{1}{2}$")	6.97 (22' 10$\frac{1}{2}$")
Finalist (1984 Olympics)	5.47 (17'11$\frac{1}{2}$")	5.91 (19'4$\frac{3}{4}$")	6.21 (20'4$\frac{1}{2}$")
World Records (1960-1985)	6.00 (19'8$\frac{1}{4}$")	6.23 (20'5$\frac{1}{4}$")	6.50 (21'4")

Note. Used with permission of Dr. James Hay.

the hop phase. Major ingredients of the step include maintenance of horizontal speed, balance during flight, and landing in a position so that maximum forces occur without sacrificing horizontal speed. Although these ingredients are the same as for the hop, problems can occur, especially in controlling forward rotations. The reason for this inevitable problem is twofold. First, because the jumper moves from one foot to another, there is no recovery leg under the hips to establish a counterrotation. During both

TAC Championship meet in Indianapolis. Compared to his 17.97-meter (58-foot decreased while the length of the step phase has increased. This contributed to a decreases the vertical velocity necessary to complete an efficient step phase.

Note. Used with permission of Dr. James Hay.

the hop and jump phases, a full hitch kick occurs with either one or both legs during flight. Any such action helps reduce the unwanted rotations about the vertical axis of the center of mass. However, the difficult step phase has no such countermotion. Second, because of the body position assumed after the step takeoff, the extending or pushing leg needs to flex, pulling the heel up near the buttocks. This detracts from the long, tall, extended position that mechanically counteracts forward rotation. Instead, the shortened position of the athlete during the step flight makes the body axis less stable to rotations about the center of mass (see Figures 5.4 and 5.5).

As they sense the rotation occurring during the step flight, many jumpers cock their lead leg back behind their hip (see Figure 5.6). This cocking action serves as a slight counter to the upper body rotation. Although the action is used by many jumpers, its effectiveness is questionable. If the cocking is necessary, it probably means the step takeoff was ineffective due to the body's forward lean. As the leg is repositioned (cocked) back behind the knee, the shoulders move forward a proportionate distance, which complicates the subsequent landing and jump takeoff.

Figure 5.5 Flight phase of the hop.

Any motion or postural position that places the shoulders ahead of the hips forces a hurried or premature landing. The ideal in-flight position is described as the "moving statue," a posture that for a time is nonrevolving and frozen in a fixed position.

The athlete should be erect and balanced and should wait patiently for the ground to come back to meet his or her foot. It is important for the entire body to remain on the parabolic flight curve as long as possible.

The step phase follows a definite sequence. Upon takeoff into the step phase, the jumper wants to maintain maximum horizontal momentum. This is achieved by keeping the angle of takeoff low and flat. The head should remain level, with the eyes focused straight ahead. If the arms are delivered in a double fashion, the thumbs should be pointed downward and the arms extended and blocked off at shoulder height. The leg thrust should be initiated with the knee and not the foot, and the knee should be driven upward to a position where the thigh is parallel to the ground. These fully blocked

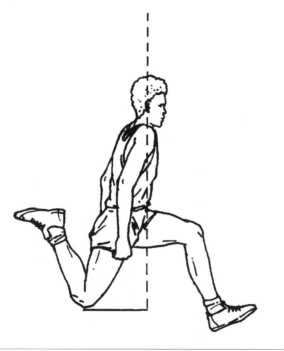

Figure 5.4 Flight phase of the step.

Figure 5.6   Backward cocking of the leg is usually caused by an improper takeoff.

knee and arm positions should be maintained in the statue position as long as possible.

The upper body, although erect, is positioned slightly ahead of the hips. This posture is necessary to help conserve forward speed into the jump phase. After release from the hop, the takeoff foot goes into a sprinter's leg recovery in which the heel moves close to the buttocks. The knee is almost fully flexed with the heel held high. The foot and leg are now in an ideal position to maximize range of motion and provide high angular momentum and force at takeoff of the jump phase.

Assuming that the jumper is using the double-arm style, while moving into the flight portion of the step, the arms should be moved out away from the body after the initial impulse of the jump. The outward position of the arms provides postural stability in the lateral direction. The objective is simply for the arms to provide balance and develop added force in the takeoff of the jump phase. To develop a large range of motion for this transference of force, the arms must be extended high back behind the body before they begin moving forward. The farther the arms are back behind the body in flight, the farther the center of mass shifts back on the parabola. This backward shift will delay the point of foot contact, which means additional distance in the step.

As the body begins to descend, the lead leg, which has been held at 90°, begins to extend out in front of the jumper. At the completion of this extension, the leg is actively pulled down and back so there is an active foot plant.

Phase 3: The Jump

The takeoff action for the jump is very similar to that for the step with the desirable addition of a swinging leg or legs upon takeoff and into the jump. As discussed earlier, the secondary rotation created by the swinging of one or both legs will counterbalance some of the upper body's forward rotation. This counterreaction allows the jumper to remain on the parabolic flight curve longer, producing a longer jump.

In the step, the landing or support foot assumes the takeoff impetus into the jump. The horizontal speed of the support phase of the step must now be converted into much more of a vertical component than was present in either the hop or the step (Gros & Kunkel, 1987). Although the jumper should attempt to increase this vertical takeoff component, it must not be emphasized at the expense of losing horizontal speed through the support and takeoff phases of the jump.

In the jump, as opposed to the two previous phases, there is a big difference in line of sight and focal direction. The chin and eyes move

Coach's Tip

During the step, the triple jumper should maintain a tall, upright posture and "ride out the flight phase." The jumper should not hurry the foot back to the ground but should wait for the ground to come to meet the foot.

Coach's Tip

Going into the jump, all remaining horizontal velocity must be directed into vertical speed.

upward at takeoff. As this is occurring, it is important to keep the chest and upper body tall and erect. However, a common problem is that the head goes back too far and pulls the body back past vertical. Any backward lean is undesirable as it causes immediate deceleration and probable braking of momentum as the foot contacts the board. During the jump, as in the other phases, strong forward momentum through the support and takeoff phases is desired. In descriptive terms, the athlete wants to *run off* the board.

The hip and leg actions of the jump closely resemble the long jump takeoff during leg compression foot release. The main difference is in the amount of horizontal speed moving into the board. In the long jump, the athlete carries a great amount of horizontal velocity into the takeoff. In the jump phase of the triple jump, a majority of this speed has been lost during the hop and step phases. To counteract this, the jumper's emphasis must be on vertical velocity. The impulse at takeoff is provided by the swinging free leg, with special attention to the motion of the double arms. Even Khristo Markov, with his extended single-arm style, brings a double-arm technique into his last phase.

Going into the jump, the swinging or free leg must also emphasize power as opposed to speed. Rather than the leg being flexed with the heel held close to the buttocks, it should swing through relatively low and long. In mechanical terms, impulse is provided with a large "time" component. The takeoff leg is loaded over a long time period due to force transferred from the actions of the free leg and arms.

To understand the impact of increasing the duration of foot contact through the three jump phases of the triple jump, we can compare actual data for Khristo Markov and Michael Conley. Markov's support time was 0.10 second in the hop, 0.13 second in the step, and 0.14 second in the jump. By comparison, Conley's support time was 0.11 second in the hop, 0.16 second in the step, and 0.17 second in the jump (Susanka, 1987).

As discussed in chapter 4 for the long jump, the flight phase of the jump is designed to control rotations and to place the body at the

Kenny Harrison

This is an illustration of Kenny Harrison's 17.5-meter (57-foot 5-inch) triple jump at the 1988 U.S. jumps. By reducing the distance of this hop, he would be able to achieve more speed in the final

Figure 5.7 The landing phase of the triple jump.

most economical position for a maximum-distance landing. At takeoff, the upper body is driven upward and forward. It is desirable to create as long an axis as possible during the flight. Keeping the head and shoulders up while extending the legs provides this desired length. In preparing to land, the athlete flexes the knees up under the hips to a position described as "standing on the knees." As the arms (which remain extended) begin to travel downward and backward in a forceful circular motion, the knees will be "kipped" forward and upward, still bent and terminating up near the chest. As the arms pass the knees, the legs are extended

so the feet are at maximum distance in front of the hips. Upon landing, one leg flexes while the other remains extended, causing the hips to spin out to the side and the athlete to land ahead of the foot marks in the sand (see Figure 5.7).

In Tables 5.2 and 5.3, Sheila Hudson's performance at the 1990 TAC meet is analyzed for speed, distances, and angles of the three phases (hop, step, and jump) of all her attempts in competition. This will allow you to compare distances achieved with the release speed of Hudson's jumps and to chart the angles achieved.

Olympic trials. The hop phase in this jump covers more distance then several of his other two phases.

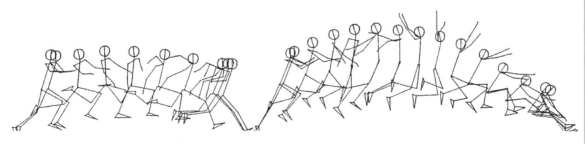

Note. Used with permission of Dr. James Hay.

Table 5.2
Distance of Sheila Hudson's Hop, Step, and Jump
During the 1990 TAC Meet

	Trial	Distance
Hop	1	4.38 m (14'4")
	2	4.78 m (15'8¼")
	3	4.94 m (16'2½")
	4	4.83 m (15'10")
	5	4.76 m (15'7¼")
	6	4.98 m (16'4")
Step	1	4.00 m (13'1½")
	2	4.09 m (13'5")
	3	4.23 m (13'10½")
	4	4.43 m (14'6¼")
	5	4.57 m (15'0")
	6	4.63 m (15'2¼")
Jump	1	5.04 m (16'5¼")
	2	4.81 m (15'9¼")
	3	4.56 m (14'11½")
	4	4.58 m (15'¼")
	5	4.88 m (16'0")
	6	4.43 m (14'6¼")

Note. Used with permission of Dr. James Hay.

Triple Jump Training Program

Workout samples for the triple jump are shown in Figures 5.8 to 5.11. There is a sample weekly workout for the general preparation, specific preparation, power development, and competition mesocycles. These are examples for a college-level athlete.

General training activities are listed in the left column of each workout. Specific activities for each day of the week (which are taken directly from the left column) are listed in the right column. Each weekly workout includes running, and emphasis is placed on strength, technical, multithrow, flexibility, coordination, and psychological areas.

Sheila Hudson

This is a sequence of Sheila Hudson's 14.07-meter (46-foot 2-inch) triple jump at the 1990 TAC earlier jumps, she was unable to achieve an accurate runway. This caused her to arrive at the phase transferred over into the step phase, which also had less velocity than in previous jumps. of the step phase.

Table 5.3
Speed, Angle, and Height of Sheila Hudson's Takeoff and Touchdown During the 1990 TAC Meet

	Trial	Speed of takeoff (m/s)	Angle of takeoff (deg)	Height of takeoff (m)	Height of touchdown (m)
Hop	1	8.68	11.1	1.00	0.95
	2	8.81	11.6	0.98	0.98
	3	8.70	13.3	0.97	0.91
	4	9.02	14.5	0.98	0.97
	5	8.93	11.9	0.98	0.92
	6	8.97	13.7	0.96	0.92
Step	1	8.15	9.4	0.97	0.94
	2	8.40	8.1	1.01	0.97
	3	7.95	10.9	0.94	0.92
	4	8.51	11.9	1.02	0.98
	5	8.64	12.6	1.00	0.95
	6	8.08	12.9	1.04	0.95
Jump	1	6.86	19.5	1.03	0.93
	2	6.78	21.2	0.98	0.91
	3	6.39	21.3	1.00	0.89
	4	6.46	21.9	1.04	0.91
	5	6.67	21.8	1.05	0.94
	6	7.01	14.8	0.97	0.89

Note. Used with permission of Dr. James Hay.

Championship in Norwalk, California. While her performance was an improvement on board with less horizontal velocity than she had in earlier jumps. The speed of the hop Excessive rotation through the frontal axis at the step takeoff also affected the distance

Note. Used with permission of Dr. James Hay.

General Preparation Workout

1. **Easy jogging**
2. **Warm-up drills:**
   (a) High leg to 50
   (b) Fast legs to 50
   (c) Cariokas
   (d) A-B-Cs to 50
   (e) Stretching
3. **Skipping:**
   (a) Standard
   (b) Power
   (c) Double arms
4. **Stadium stairs:**
   (a) Sprinting up
   (b) Springing down
   (c) Hopping up
       (1) Single leg
       (2) Double legs
   (d) Hopping down
       (1) Single leg
       (2) Double legs
5. **Power runs:**
   (a) Hills
   (b) Belts
6. **Downhills:**
   (a) General
   (b) With takeoff
7. **Speed bounding:**
   (a) Single leg
   (b) Double legs
   (c) RR-LL
   (d) H-S-S-S-H
   (e) From 8 steps
8. **Power bounding:**
   (a) Single leg
   (b) Double legs
   (c) RR-LL
9. **Landing drills:**
   (a) Split
   (b) Alternate
   (c) Standing on knees
   (d) Full
10. **Penultimate step drills:**
    (a) 8 steps
    (b) 4 steps

11. **Hurdle hops:**
    (a) Flat
    (b) Box to 5 hurdles
    (c) Box to 8 hurdles
12. **Coach's mark to takeoff timing**
13. **Simulated runway:**
    (a) Full
    (b) 8 steps
    (c) 6 steps
14. **Weights:**
    (a) Special
        (1) Clean & jerk
        (2) Single-leg squats
        (3) Weighted vest
        (4) Lunges
    (b) Circuit
    (c) Power strength (general)
    (d) Arm drills
15. **Running sets:**
    (a) 40
    (b) 50
    (c) 60
    (d) 70
    (e) 80
    (f) 100
    (g) 110
    (h) 150
    (i) 180
    (j) 200
    (k) 300
    (l) 322
    (m) 400
    (n) 500
    (o) 550
    (p) 600
    (q) 800
    (r) 1,000
16. **Hurdles:** (same as above)
17. **Timed drop-downs:**
    (a) 20-30-20
    (b) 20-40-20
    (c) 20-50-20
    (d) 20-60

(continued)

Figure 5.8   Sample triple jump workout during the general preparation mesocycle.

18. **Running drills:**
    (a) Backward
    (b) Circle
    (c) Figure 8
    (d) Side hills
    (e) Pop-ups

19. **Boxes:**
    (a) 14-16' bounding R-L-R-L;
       16-18' bounding R-L-R-L
    (b) RR-LL
    (c) Single leg through both legs
    (d) **HJ drills**
       (1) Table jumping
       (2) Ground-to-box-to-ground jumping
       (3) Ground-to-low-box jumping
    (e) **LJ drills**
       (1) Ground-to-box-to-ground jumping
       (2) Ground-to-low-box jumping

20. Meet with coach

21 **Films:**
    (a) Study session
    (b) To be filmed

22. Rehabilitation

23. Precompetition warm-up/check marks

24. Pool

25. **Medicine ball series:**
    (a) Double arms
    (b) Abdominal

26. Running circuit

27. Distance run

Legend of
Work-to-Rest Ratios

Monday

(1 to 1,200) (stretch) (2 a-b-c-d × 6 ea.)
(3a × 2 to 400 ea.)
(15j × 8 gradual drop-downs -
2-min recovery)
(cooldown)

Tuesday

(1 to 1,200) (stretch) (2 a-b-c-d × 5 ea.)
(3a with double arm × 6 to 80)
(13 full runs with count – timed last 4 steps)
(7-8 to 80 × 4 ea. leg) (7d to 80 × 4)
(18a to 80 × 4) (14 absolute strength)
Special

Wednesday

(1 to 800) (stretch) (2 a-b-c-d × 5 ea.)
(a-b-c-d from 1/2 runway × 4-6 ea.)
(21 × 2 of ea. drill) (4a × 4 steady)
(6a to 80 × 8)
(cooldown)

Thursday

(1 to 2 mi) (stretch) (2 a-b-c-d × 5 ea.)
(3 × with double arm × 3 to 60)
(14 absolute strength)
Special

Friday

Basketball

Saturday

Rest

Sunday

(14 absolute strength)
Special

Figure 5.8   *(continued)*

Specific Preparation Workout

1. **Easy jogging**
2. **Warm-up drills:**
   (a) High leg to 50
   (b) Fast legs to 50
   (c) Cariokas
   (d) A-B-Cs to 50
   (e) Stretching
3. **Skipping:**
   (a) Standard
   (b) Power
   (c) Double arms
4. **Stadium stairs:**
   (a) Sprinting up
   (b) Springing down
   (c) Hopping up
       (1) Single leg
       (2) Double legs
   (d) Hopping down
       (1) Single leg
       (2) Double legs
5. **Power runs:**
   (a) Hills
   (b) Belts
6. **Downhills:**
   (a) General
   (b) With takeoff
7. **Speed bounding:**
   (a) Single leg
   (b) Double legs
   (c) RR-LL
   (d) H-S-S-S-H
   (e) From 8 steps
8. **Power bounding:**
   (a) Single leg
   (b) Double legs
   (c) RR-LL
9. **Landing drills:**
   (a) Split
   (b) Alternate
   (c) Standing on knees
   (d) Full
10. **Penultimate step drills:**
    (a) 8 steps
    (b) 4 steps
11. **Hurdle hops:**
    (a) Flat
    (b) Box to 5 hurdles
    (c) Box to 8 hurdles
12. Coach's mark to takeoff timing
13. **Simulated runway:**
    (a) Full
    (b) 8 steps
    (c) 6 steps
14. **Weights:**
    (a) Special
        (1) Clean & jerk
        (2) Single-leg squats
        (3) Weighted vest
        (4) Lunges
    (b) Circuit
    (c) Power strength (general)
    (d) Arm drills
15. **Running sets:**
    (a) 40
    (b) 50
    (c) 60
    (d) 70
    (e) 80
    (f) 100
    (g) 110
    (h) 150
    (i) 180
    (j) 200
    (k) 300
    (l) 322
    (m) 400
    (n) 500
    (o) 550
    (p) 600
    (q) 800
    (r) 1,000
16. **Hurdles:** (same as above)
17. **Timed drop-downs:**
    (a) 20-30-20
    (b) 20-40-20
    (c) 20-50-20
    (d) 20-60

(continued)

Figure 5.9 Sample triple jump workout during the specific preparation mesocycle.

18. **Running drills:**
    (a) Backward
    (b) Circle
    (c) Figure 8
    (d) Side hills
    (e) Pop-ups
19. **Boxes:**
    (a) 14-16' bounding R-L-R-L;
        16-18' bounding R-L-R-L
    (b) RR-LL
    (c) Single leg through both legs
    (d) **HJ drills**
        (1) Table jumping
        (2) Ground-to-box-to-ground jumping
        (3) Ground-to-low-box jumping
    (e) **LJ drills**
        (1) Ground-to-box-to-ground jumping
        (2) Ground-to-low-box jumping
20. Meet with coach
21 **Films:**
    (a) Study session
    (b) To be filmed
22. Rehabilitation
23. Precompetition warm-up/check marks
24. Pool
25. **Medicine ball series:**
    (a) Double arms
    (b) Abdominal
26. Running circuit
27. Distance run

Legend of Work-to-Rest Ratios

Monday

(1 to 800) (stretch) (2 a-b-c-d × 4 ea.)
(15c × 6 steady) (15k × 3) (15h × 4)
(cooldown)

Tuesday

(1 to 2 mi) (stretch) (2 a-b-c-d × 5)
(13a × 6)
(14 special cycle)
(cooldown)

Wednesday

(1 to 1,200) (stretch) (2 a-b-c-d × 6 ea.)
(outside to turf – 70 to 80 – 14 ground contacts)
(emphasis on arms) (21)
(8a to 100 alternate × 5)
(15e × 6) (cooldown)

Thursday

(light warm-up) (2 a-b-c-d as you feel)
(14 special cycle)
(lateral bench hop test × 2)

Friday

(distance run to 5 mi)
(6a @ 3⁄4 effort to 60 × 6)

Saturday

Rest—no competition
To test for body fat

Sunday

(14 special cycle)

Figure 5.9 *(continued)*

Power Development Workout

1. **Easy jogging**
2. **Warm-up drills:**
   (a) High leg to 50
   (b) Fast legs to 50
   (c) Cariokas
   (d) A-B-Cs to 50
   (e) Stretching
3. **Skipping:**
   (a) Standard
   (b) Power
   (c) Double arms
4. **Stadium stairs:**
   (a) Sprinting up
   (b) Springing down
   (c) Hopping up
      (1) Single leg
      (2) Double legs
   (d) Hopping down
      (1) Single leg
      (2) Double legs
5. **Power runs:**
   (a) Hills
   (b) Belts
6. **Downhills:**
   (a) General
   (b) With takeoff
7. **Speed bounding:**
   (a) Single leg
   (b) Double legs
   (c) RR-LL
   (d) H-S-S-S-H
   (e) From 8 steps
8. **Power bounding:**
   (a) Single leg
   (b) Double legs
   (c) RR-LL
9. **Landing drills:**
   (a) Split
   (b) Alternate
   (c) Standing on knees
   (d) Full
10. **Penultimate step drills:**
    (a) 8 steps
    (b) 4 steps
11. **Hurdle hops:**
    (a) Flat
    (b) Box to 5 hurdles
    (c) Box to 8 hurdles
12. Coach's mark to takeoff timing
13. **Simulated runway:**
    (a) Full
    (b) 8 steps
    (c) 6 steps
14. **Weights:**
    (a) Special
       (1) Clean & jerk
       (2) Single-leg squats
       (3) Weighted vest
       (4) Lunges
    (b) Circuit
    (c) Power strength (general)
    (d) Arm drills
15. **Running sets:**
    (a) 40
    (b) 50
    (c) 60
    (d) 70
    (e) 80
    (f) 100
    (g) 110
    (h) 150
    (i) 180
    (j) 200
    (k) 300
    (l) 322
    (m) 400
    (n) 500
    (o) 550
    (p) 600
    (q) 800
    (r) 1,000
16. **Hurdles:** (same as above)
17. **Timed drop-downs:**
    (a) 20-30-20
    (b) 20-40-20
    (c) 20-50-20
    (d) 20-60

(continued)

Figure 5.10 Sample triple jump workout during the power development mesocycle.

18. **Running drills:**
    (a) Backward
    (b) Circle
    (c) Figure 8
    (d) Side hills
    (e) Pop-ups

19. **Boxes:**
    (a) 14-16' bounding R-L-R-L;
        16-18' bounding R-L-R-L
    (b) RR-LL
    (c) Single leg through both legs
    (d) **HJ drills**
        (1) Table jumping
        (2) Ground-to-box-to-ground jumping
        (3) Ground-to-low-box jumping
    (e) **LJ drills**
        (1) Ground-to-box-to-ground jumping
        (2) Ground-to-low-box jumping

20. Meet with coach

21 **Films:**
    (a) Study session
    (b) To be filmed

22. Rehabilitation

23. Precompetition warm-up/check marks

24. Pool

25. **Medicine ball series:**
    (a) Double arms
    (b) Abdominal

26. Running circuit

27. Distance run

Legend of Work-to-Rest Ratios

Monday

(1 to 2 mi) (stretch)
(5a to 180 × 7 drop-downs)
(cooldown)

Tuesday

(1 to 2 mi) (stretch) (3b × 4 to 100)
(14 outdoor comp prep)

Wednesday

(1 to 2 mi) (stretch) (3b × 6 to 80)
(15j × 4) (6a × 8 do not overstride)

Thursday

(1 to 1 mi) (stretch) (2 a-b-c-d × 8)
(3b × 6 to 60) (18a × 6 to 50)
(4a × 4 – 4b × 4)
(14 posted)

Friday

(1 to 1 mi) (stretch) (2 a-b-c-d × 6)
(3b – double arm 4 to 80)
(18 – quick feet in ladder)
(7d × 100 × 4)
(cooldown)

Saturday

Rest

Sunday

(14 posted)

Figure 5.10   *(continued)*

Competition Workout

1. **Easy jogging**
2. **Warm-up drills:**
   - (a) High leg to 50
   - (b) Fast legs to 50
   - (c) Cariokas
   - (d) A-B-Cs to 50
   - (e) Stretching
3. **Skipping:**
   - (a) Standard
   - (b) Power
   - (c) Double arms
4. **Stadium stairs:**
   - (a) Sprinting up
   - (b) Springing down
   - (c) Hopping up
       - (1) Single leg
       - (2) Double legs
   - (d) Hopping down
       - (1) Single leg
       - (2) Double legs
5. **Power runs:**
   - (a) Hills
   - (b) Belts
6. **Downhills:**
   - (a) General
   - (b) With takeoff
7. **Speed bounding:**
   - (a) Single leg
   - (b) Double legs
   - (c) RR-LL
   - (d) H-S-S-S-H
   - (e) From 8 steps
8. **Power bounding:**
   - (a) Single leg
   - (b) Double legs
   - (c) RR-LL
9. **Landing drills:**
   - (a) Split
   - (b) Alternate
   - (c) Standing on knees
   - (d) Full
10. **Penultimate step drills:**
    - (a) 8 steps
    - (b) 4 steps
11. **Hurdle hops:**
    - (a) Flat
    - (b) Box to 5 hurdles
    - (c) Box to 8 hurdles
12. Coach's mark to takeoff timing
13. **Simulated runway:**
    - (a) Full
    - (b) 8 steps
    - (c) 6 steps
14. **Weights:**
    - (a) Special
        - (1) Clean & jerk
        - (2) Single-leg squats
        - (3) Weighted vest
        - (4) Lunges
    - (b) Circuit
    - (c) Power strength (general)
    - (d) Arm drills
15. **Running sets:**
    - (a) 40
    - (b) 50
    - (c) 60
    - (d) 70
    - (e) 80
    - (f) 100
    - (g) 110
    - (h) 150
    - (i) 180
    - (j) 200
    - (k) 300
    - (l) 322
    - (m) 400
    - (n) 500
    - (o) 550
    - (p) 600
    - (q) 800
    - (r) 1,000
16. **Hurdles:** (same as above)
17. **Timed drop-downs:**
    - (a) 20-30-20
    - (b) 20-40-20
    - (c) 20-50-20
    - (d) 20-60

(continued)

Figure 5.11   Sample triple jump workout during the competition mesocycle.

18. **Running drills:**
    (a) Backward
    (b) Circle
    (c) Figure 8
    (d) Side hills
    (e) Pop-ups

19. **Boxes:**
    (a) 14-16' bounding R-L-R-L;
        16-18' bounding R-L-R-L
    (b) RR-LL
    (c) Single leg through both legs
    (d) **HJ drills**
        (1) Table jumping
        (2) Ground-to-box-to-ground jumping
        (3) Ground-to-low-box jumping
    (e) **LJ drills**
        (1) Ground-to-box-to-ground jumping
        (2) Ground-to-low-box jumping

20. Meet with coach

21 **Films:**
    (a) Study session
    (b) To be filmed

22. Rehabilitation

23. Precompetition warm-up/check marks

24. Pool

25. **Medicine ball series:**
    (a) Double arms
    (b) Abdominal

26. Running circuit

27. Distance run

Legend of Work-to-Rest Ratios

Tuesday

(easy running) (stretching)
(drills as you feel)
(13a × 5)
(cooldown)

Wednesday

(full warm-up)
(17a × 6)

Thursday

Travel to championship meet
Check out facilities
(13 × 3 check) (9 a-b-d short run)
(cooldown)

Friday

Rest

Saturday

Competition

Sunday

Rest

Monday

(easy running) (stretching)
(all drills as you feel)
(15e × 5) (6b full count system)
(cooldown)

Figure 5.11 *(continued)*

Chapter 6
High Jump

The high jumping event underwent a major evolution in the late 1960s when Dick Fosbury rose to prominence using his now-famous back layout style. From then on, more and more athletes began to use the flop technique instead of the earlier straddle technique popularized by the great Valery Brumel, who had the distinction of jumping 7 feet 4-1/2 inches from a dirt approach and landing in wood shavings.

The modern-day style employed by almost all American and international jumpers was introduced by Fosbury, of course, but gained popularity for reasons other than this individual athlete's success. The early straddle technique required the athlete to be physically strong, as were Brumel and others who were at the top. Young jumpers who emulated them

Keys to High Jumping

- Develop an effective run-up, including proper speed, angular momentum, and hip height throughout the run

- Get in a position to transfer the hips from a horizontal to a vertical direction without disrupting the acceleration and tempo of the run

- Align body posture so that at ground release, the jumper rotates forward and laterally at the same time ensuring that the speed of rotation is adequate to get the jumper's body over and around the bar as quickly as possible

attempted to do what their role models were doing—run very fast and, just before takeoff, try to get as low as possible. But most of these young athletes found they didn't have the leg strength they needed, and injuries to the knee became abundant. At that time, only the naturally strong achieved much success in the high jump.

Then Fosbury's technique came along. It looked fun and intriguing to emerging athletes, and youngsters soon learned they could achieve success even though they were not particularly strong. In addition, big, soft landing pits were becoming available, and the jumper could now land on the shoulders and back safely. As a result, nearly all jumpers were becoming floppers.

The flop high jump is unique among the jumping techniques. Unlike pole vaulters and horizontal jumpers, the high jumper runs with less speed during the approach. Flop high jumpers are also the only ones to follow a curved path prior to takeoff, providing significant technical challenges for both coach and athlete.

In high jump coaching, doing the obvious is not necessarily what's best. The obvious is to coach what happens on top of the bar, but once the jumper leaves the ground, very little can be done to change the outcome of the jump. On the other hand, almost everything that happens in the air is determined during the approach. Thus, coaching goals for the high jump should almost exclusively be devoted to what the athlete does while on the ground, from the approach start until the actual takeoff.

If high jump technique is correct on the ground, the jumper doesn't need to worry about what happens over the bar. Natural manipulations occur during flight, stemming mostly from the action-reaction principle (Newton's third law). As the jumper becomes more experienced, subtle in-flight body adjustments are learned that make the athlete more effective. The main thing to remember is that the flight path is set while the jumper is applying force to the ground. That's why we strongly recommend to coaches that 90% of all training time be spent on the technical aspects of the run-up.

Approach

Several important concepts must be visualized by the coach and athlete when thinking about the total approach. These are listed below as objectives and will be dealt with specifically in the remainder of the chapter.

First, the athlete must develop a consistent tempo and stride pattern from the beginning to end of the approach. In addition, each jumper needs to determine the optimum speed that can be carried into the takeoff. This is determined primarily by leg strength and upright posture through the penultimate stride. A jumper must never slow down prior to takeoff.

The absolute key to an effective jump is the ability to "load" the muscles of the plant leg. Every technique that adds to this muscle loading must be employed. Incorporating a free-swinging leg and good utilization of both arms provide a lot of extra force to the takeoff leg.

Coach's Tip

If an athlete develops only one technique well, it must be the creation of impulse via a loaded takeoff leg.

Finally, the jumper must pay attention to backward and lateral posture at takeoff. These two factors alone will give the jumper a vertical takeoff position.

A basic premise concerning runway speed is that, regardless of ability, the athlete needs only to generate sufficient speed to adequately load the quadriceps muscles of the takeoff leg to make the transition from the horizontal to the vertical direction. If the athlete runs too fast, the leg will buckle and vertical transition will be impossible. If the athlete runs too slowly, the stretch reflexes will not be adequately stimulated. Too little approach velocity will not provide enough energy to complete the necessary rotations over the bar, let alone enough speed to carry the athlete into the pit. Obviously, the skill level of the athlete will dictate the amount of effective speed. You cannot expect a young athlete to carry nearly as much speed as a strong, mature jumper.

At some point, it is wise for the jumper to learn the double-arm action. This technique is difficult to learn because it must blend into the runway without hindering speed, but it is very important to generating force for additional leg loading.

Setting Up the Approach Run

Historically, there are three methods of performing a flop approach run. Basic to all three methods is the necessity for a curved run with a lateral lean away from the bar at takeoff. Throughout the relatively short evolution of the flop-style jump, there has been considerable experimentation to find the ultimate takeoff position and consistent approach. In the beginning, Fosbury used a constant curved approach with his eight-step, right-footed takeoff. His actual approach looked like the one depicted in Figure 6.1.

This approach, although functional for Fosbury in setting his world record, had potential problems. On the positive side, it provided a constant curve and, when run properly, allowed him to lean away from the bar and be vertical at the instant of takeoff. On the negative side, because of the constant curve, he was unable to produce a lot of speed. More important, he was unable to show consistency of momentum from one jump to another or from one facility to another. A difficult aspect of the run for a young jumper is simply making the transition from the straight-ahead run into the curve. It is even more difficult to remain on a constant curve, as was the case for Fosbury.

In recent years, an improvement on the constant curved approach has become somewhat of a trademark for current jumpers. This relatively simple and consistent means of approaching the bar is called the "J" approach because it resembles the letter J (see Figure 6.2).

The primary advantage of this style of approach is that it has a constant, predetermined pattern starting a specific distance (reference point) measured out from the standard. In addition, momentum is easily established during the straight portion of the run,

Coach's Tip

The most important aspect of the curved approach is foot placement on the next to last step. If the foot placement is aligned with the takeoff foot, the jumper maintains a lateral lean. If the foot placement is out of alignment, the jumper's shoulders move into the bar and a vertical takeoff is impossible.

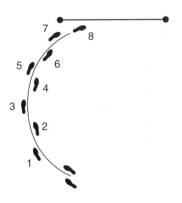

Figure 6.1 Fosbury's original eight-step curved approach.

so acceleration should definitely occur. There is also consistency when the athlete moves off the straight into the curve. At the point where the outside foot hits the ground (at either step 5 or step 7), the foot is simply rotated inward. This begins the curve and makes the transition smooth (see Figure 6.3). Once the actual curve has begun, the focus should be on achieving a tall, upright posture and rapid leg turnover.

Using the J setup is like following a precise road map en route to the takeoff. The jumper strives for the following:

- A constant distance from the bar
- A constant, even curve to follow
- Exact placement of each foot throughout the run
- A constant tempo acceleration from start to finish
- A constant feeling of pushing the hips and body out away from the curve
- An exact takeoff spot with the body erect but with a lateral lean *away* from the bar

Finally, as a jumper progresses and improves, the run can be further modified to provide increases in speed and more efficient loading of the takeoff leg. With this in mind, a possible alternative for the veteran jumper is a version of the constant curved approach called the "hook" because it resembles a fish hook (see Figure 6.4). The advantage of this approach is that it allows the jumper to make an easy, smooth transition from the straight to the curved portion of the run. The jumper has the feeling of running a constant curve throughout the approach yet there is no tendency to slow down.

The hook approach is a way to blend horizontal momentum into a productive body posture going into the penultimate and eventual takeoff steps. With the hook, lateral lean occurs naturally if the athlete remains on the curve. Everything—momentum, speed, and lean—should happen gradually (see Figure 6.4).

A disadvantage of the hook is the potential for the athlete to get out too wide on either step 6 or step 8. Unless the athlete is constantly on guard, this approach can end

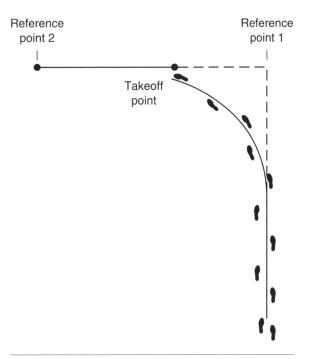

Figure 6.2   The 10-step J approach.

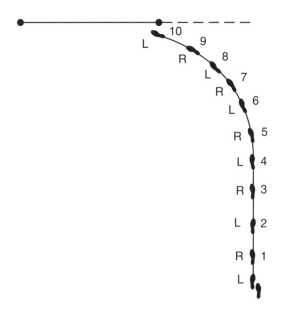

Figure 6.3   When the outside foot hits the ground on the fifth step, the foot is then rotated inward.

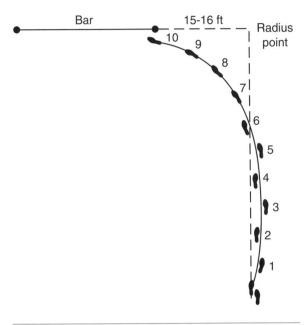

Figure 6.4 The hook approach.

up being the old Fosbury circular approach and the benefits will be outweighed by potential inconsistencies. Although the radius point (called the reference point) becomes almost constant with the experienced jumper (15-16 feet), experimentation is necessary to find what the jumper can handle (i.e., the ability to accelerate throughout the run-up yet remain on a curve). The general rule of thumb for setting the radius is the slower the athlete, the narrower the radius; the faster, stronger, and more controlled the athlete, the wider the radius. However, an inexperienced jumper is well advised to begin with a wider curve.

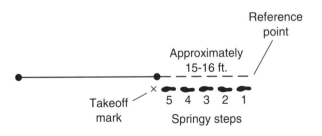

Figure 6.5 To establish an individual curve distance, stand at the takeoff mark and take five springy steps from it.

A simple way to establish an individual curve distance is to stand at the predetermined takeoff mark and take five "springy" steps away from the mark (see Figure 6.5).

Stride and Tempo During Approach

The acceleration pattern is simply to make the approach a constant acceleration from the beginning of the run until takeoff. We usually think of acceleration as having two components: stride length and stride frequency, better known as *turnover*. In all approach runs, stride frequency must increase constantly up to and through the takeoff phase of the jump. Stride length, on the other hand, is best described as a gradual progression through the penultimate stride. This longer stride allows the athlete's hips to lower slightly, allowing the jumper to begin making the transition from horizontal to vertical velocity.

To achieve the desired acceleration pattern, a tempo must be developed for each individual. One way of developing tempo is for the athlete to use a counting system. Our jumpers generally rely on either a 10- or 12-step approach. Our preference is a standing start approach, which is especially helpful for the beginner. A walk-in, run-in or bound-in approach will introduce many inaccuracies to an already difficult run-up. A consistent stationary start will result in a run-up with good, accurate acceleration.

A helpful coaching technique is to assign even numbers to the takeoff foot (i.e., 2-4-6-8-10-12) and to begin the run with the jumping or takeoff foot situated on a check mark. As the nontakeoff foot leaves the ground and subsequently contacts the ground, it becomes step 1. Thus, the first ground contact of the takeoff foot becomes step 2, and thereafter each step count of the takeoff foot is an even number, eventually becoming either count 10 or count 12 at takeoff.

As the athlete develops a count and a rhythm, the tempo simply quickens as he or she progresses toward takeoff. There must be no slowing, blocking, or chopping of strides prior to foot release at takeoff.

Our experience has shown that a 10-step approach provides an economy of controlled speed for the majority of jumpers. However, some jumpers are using 12- and 14-step approaches. Although some are making effective use of the added length, others are generating too much speed and inconsistency for an effective transfer from horizontal speed to a good vertical takeoff position.

The athlete's primary objective in the run-up is to make every approach exactly the same. Contrary to what some may believe, distance from the bar and speed of approach should remain constant on all jumps, regardless of bar height or conditions. Thus, it is important to establish a starting check mark.

To simplify the run-up, a beginning jumper should use a 10-step approach until he or she has developed consistency and has become a good jumper. Unless the jumper is experienced, increasing the number of steps only complicates the approach and usually leads to decel-eration rather than the desired gradual buildup of speed.

Posture and body position are important but are often forgotten in coaching the high jumper. If the athlete is running properly, posture is basically a product of acceleration. As the jumper starts the run, acceleration begins, causing a proportionate forward lean. As the jumper reaches maximum speed, the body naturally assumes an upright position. The jumper should never bend from the waist or lean back during the approach run. (Remember, a backward lean during a run is caused by unwanted deceleration.)

The athlete should start the approach with a solid push down and back off the starting position to establish momentum. As inertia is gradually overcome, the stride begins to turn over more quickly, much like the wheels of an old steam locomotive as it builds up speed. As the stride quickens and lengthens, the body becomes more and more erect until the head, shoulders, and trunk are in a straight

Hollis Conway

This is a biomechanical analysis of a high jump with 2.25-meters (7-feet 4-1/2 inches) clearance of hips and the arm action. The lateral lean is also interesting.

line perpendicular to the ground. Thus, the functions of the run-up are to develop adequate speed and tempo and to produce the most effective body posture with which to leave the ground.

In developing our jumpers, we spend a lot of time counting out the steps of the approach and analyzing what occurs in each of the different phases. For example, in a typical 10-step approach, the curve begins on step 5 and the arm action is initiated on step 8. This method allows us to pinpoint for the athlete the specific step during the runway where problems are occurring and to recommend solutions.

As mentioned earlier, rhythm and tempo can be developed by using the count system. The count method also makes it easier to classify and concentrate on specific techniques during the total approach run. A coach who is tuned in to the constant tempo buildup of a jumper can hear as well as watch the run. The foot strike rhythm starts with a slow to constant increase in speed through the first 8 steps, then culminates with a "da-da" sound on steps 9 and 10.

Typically, one of two problems tends to occur at the 8th, 9th, and 10th steps. The jumper either begins to "back off" (reduce speed) over these three steps or gets ready for the "big one" and lengthens out of proportion the stride length of one or all three steps.

From count step 1 through step 6 or 7, there should be a gradual increase of stride length as well as tempo. At the transition, steps 8 through 10, there should be a change of stride length. The penultimate step (step 9) should lengthen by 6 to 8 inches, and the last step (step 10) should shorten by nearly the same amount. The key to speed in the runway is to very deliberately *run through* without slowing or backing away from the bar.

Note that the speed through the first five to seven steps of the run is basically developed by stride length and momentum. Then, during the final steps of the approach, speed is influenced by turnover or frequency. The foot

by Hollis Conway. The last three steps and jump sequence are shown. Note the height

Note. Used with permission of Dr. Jesus Dapena and the United States Olympic Committee.

Coach's Tip

To be effective, a jumper must be as fast and as low as possible going into the next to last step. Being too fast or too low will cause the leg to buckle. Constant effort to develop these two components is the key to success.

strike of these final steps (other than the take-off) should be directly under the hips. The legs must recover high with the foot near the buttocks and should not be extended back behind the hips.

Transition From Run to Takeoff

As in any jump, in moving from run to take-off, the athlete strives to convert horizontal speed into a large vertical impulse. This adjustment during the run is called the *transition*. An effective transition (one that causes little or no slowing prior to takeoff) is one of the most difficult skills to learn and apply. The trick is to develop adequate speed to lower the center of mass so the hips can be redirected from horizontal to vertical. An analysis of many high jumpers shows the angle of take-off to be around 48° for the good jumpers and 52° for the great ones (Paklin, Kostavanova, Sotomayor).

The purpose of the transition phase is to develop maximum vertical velocity without slowing speed in the horizontal direction.

Impulse (force × time) is what determines vertical velocity. Impulse is the technical term for loading the takeoff leg and is the most

important element of a good jump. The jumper seeks to employ the stretch reflexes of the quadriceps muscles to their fullest. The more quickly these muscles are forced to stretch, the more powerful will be the contraction or leg extension. Because impulse is equal to the force applied multiplied by the time of application, our goal is to decrease time and increase force, thus providing maximum vertical velocity. The longer the force can be applied from a low position to a high position, the greater the vertical velocity will be. This is a confusing and even controversial theory, but the idea is to capture the best of both—force and time. So how does the athlete achieve a low hip position without slowing? There are two factors that make it possible.

First, during the penultimate step, flexion of the knee and ankle occurs. Foot contact must be directly under the hips and not out in front. The good penultimate is initiated by an incomplete leg push off the third stride out from takeoff. During this foot strike, ground contact is flatter than normal. The result is a subtle lowering of the hips but without any slowing.

The second component of hip lowering occurs naturally as the athlete leans *away* while running the curve. This lateral lean causes the hips to lower with no undue slowing (see Figure 6.6). However, if the athlete leaves the curve at any time, the hips move from a low to a high position. This undesirable tendency usually occurs on either step 9 of a 10-step approach or step 11 of a 12-step approach.

Leg loading is the most important factor in high jumping. We are concerned with causing the stretch reflex to occur over the shortest possible time. This means as little knee flexion as possible and a solid flat-footed takeoff with the center of mass (hips) slightly behind the takeoff foot. The arm motions and the foot strike of the free leg should be simultaneous with the extension of the takeoff leg. This timing of the free-moving limbs transfers additional force into the ground, and due to the action-reaction principle, the ground returns equal force back into the jumper's hips.

Perhaps the biggest advantage of the flop-style jump over other high jump styles is that it utilizes a curved run-up. The reason for this is the lateral lean (away) from the bar that occurs just prior to liftoff. At the instant of liftoff, the lateral lean can set up a near-perfect vertical position because the forces at work are concentrated in a vertical direction as opposed to the eccentric forces experienced with the straddle-type jump.

As the athlete leans into the curve in an attempt to counteract centrifugal force, impulse is initiated even though the takeoff leg is not flexed. This is due to the center of mass (hips) moving from a low position (leaning away from the bar) to a more vertical or upright position (see Figure 6.6). The greater the lateral lean, the lower the hip position, creating more time to impart vertical impulse at takeoff.

With the curved run, two components of angular momentum also come into play. First, there is a forward somersaulting action caused by checking the speed of the straight run. Second, there is a lateral somersaulting action caused by the lean away from the bar. As a result, the jumper's body leaves the ground in a tangent (straight line) established by a combination of these lateral and horizontal components.

Ultimately, the athlete who develops the most angular momentum, either horizontal or lateral, will rotate along the bar at a faster speed. Faster rotations create fewer difficulties at bar clearance.

The emphasis in running the curve should be on maintaining the maximum momentum originally established during steps 1 through 8 of the runway count.

Despite the advantages of the curved approach, problems can occur during its implementation. Too often jumpers think they are running the curve when in reality they are "stepping out" and losing important lean en route to the jump. To maintain a constant curve, the jumper must place each foot directly on a line beneath the hips that bisects the body. In other words, the footsteps must follow a very narrow curved line.

During a normal running stride, foot placement is directly under the hip joint of the striding leg. In the flop run-up, where the objective is to be on a curve, the jumper needs to place the foot in the mid-line between the hips. Figure 6.7a shows the athlete's hip-wide foot placement. If this placement were used in a curved approach, the athlete would actually be stepping out of the curve.

Most coaches think the curve should be initiated on step 6 of the approach, but we do not share this view. We believe the athlete should begin to transition into the curve with an inward rotation of step 5 (the outside foot). High jumpers who initiate the curve with the inside foot (step 6) usually develop a tendency to step out of the tight circular line that is necessary for good alignment.

Takeoff

The amount of force a jumper directs into the ground is delivered back to the jumper by the ground. This is due to the law of action-

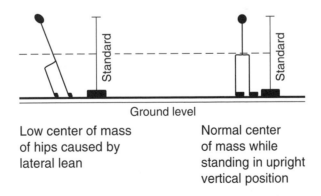

Figure 6.6 Raising hips from low to high increases the force × time for extra impulse.

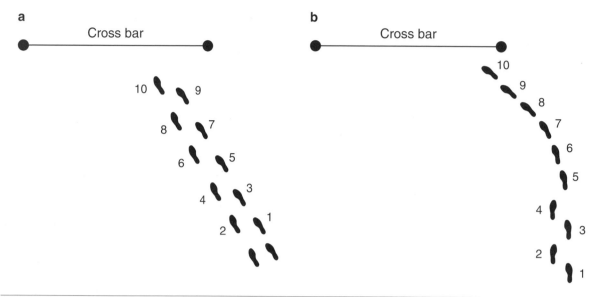

Figure 6.7   If an athlete used hip-wide foot placement (a) he would step out of the curve (b).

Doug Nordquist

This is a biomechanical analysis of a high jump with a 2.33-meter (7-foot 7-1/4-inch) clearance his height of hips, arm action, and lateral lean with those of Hollis Conway.

Coach's Tip

The sequences that are observed while the athlete is airborne are, for the most part, created at take-off. The major coaching emphasis must be directed at ground activity.

reaction: for every force exerted there is an equal counteracting force. Until now, we have been concerned with forces created by speed of the run, angular momentum, and muscle loading. Next we'll look at how the timing of the free limbs of the body can transfer additional

forces into the ground. Of the three available limbs, the swinging leg, because of its mass, has the most potential for developing force.

"Power" jumping and "speed" jumping are terms commonly used to describe various styles of flop high jumping. A good way to differentiate these styles is according to the speed of the free leg as it moves off the last step of the jump. Either the leg is shortened by placing the heel on or near the buttocks, or the leg is kept fairly straight to the point where the toe may even drag as it swings through. Although some skill is required to move the short "fast" (speed) leg through, both the long and short swings have more to do with hip height (leg flexion) and stride length over the last two steps of the approach. For clarification, in this instance, we are talking about hip height associated with support leg flexion and not with lateral lean.

Mechanically, the jumper can shorten the lead swinging leg by placing the heel of the foot on the buttocks. The more forcefully the athlete

by Doug Nordquist. The last three steps and the jump sequence are shown. Compare

Note. Used with permission of Dr. Jesus Dapena and the United States Olympic Committee.

pushes off the ground, the shorter the leg recovery. This occurs naturally and is similar to the high-recovery leg of a fast-running sprinter. As the leg moves forward into the takeoff, it stops near hip height. This stopping or blocking, as it is more commonly called, has the capability of unweighting the jumper. This, coupled with the ground force established by the fast upward swing of the leg, makes the jump more efficient.

A long lead leg will develop considerable momentum, but it is difficult to transfer this force as it is usually related to a deceleration of approach speed and is not characterized by a forceful run-through. It is more of a vertical lifting action. The long leg technique does allow for a longer generation of force over the takeoff foot. As stated earlier, this concept can develop much vertical force, and many long-lead-leg jumpers are having a great success, including Javier Sotomayor, the current world record holder.

Although not as important as the lead leg, the arms also have the potential to substantially increase the height of a jump. When moving upward with high speed, they, too, exert a compressing force down the body and into the ground. If this upward speed is suddenly checked or blocked, an unweighting effect occurs. This is called blocking. There is some question as to the effectiveness of this upward arm block and how much it contributes to a jump. In most cases, the jumper is off the ground before a block occurs.

The important factor for the arms is simply that they move upward in a vertical direction and not into the plane of the bar. It is common knowledge that vigorous use of the arms increases jumping efficiency. However, the problem for the jumper is what to do during the run-up to maintain horizontal speed while preparing the arms to do their job.

The key to an effective double-arm takeoff is to eliminate any slowing or hesitation when preparing to set up the arm action. Just as there must be constant motion of the arms and legs while hurdling, jumpers strive for the same motion during their approach run. One way the athlete is able to develop the double-arm technique is to run naturally as a sprinter

through count step 7. As the left foot moves into the 8th step, the right arm (left-legged jumper) naturally moves forward with the left foot. Instead of moving back as it normally would, on the 9th step, the right arm moves across the chest (similar to a swimmer doing the breast stroke). As the jumper moves into the last step (step 10), both arms come together behind the body to time up with the leading knee. It is important for the hips and shoulders to be separated (hips toward the far standard and shoulders rotated outward away from the bar). This increases muscle stretch through the back and trunk, thus turning the back toward the bar. Our coaching key is for the left or outside arm to drag behind the right.

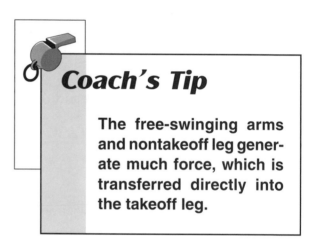

Coach's Tip

The free-swinging arms and nontakeoff leg generate much force, which is transferred directly into the takeoff leg.

Another method that yields good results for the double-arm action is to use a "run-through" position of the arms, meaning there is no attempt to gather the arm(s) in front of the body. Instead the jumper attempts to maintain a normal running action until step 9. The inside (right) arm runs through the forward position but is delayed momentarily in its backward movement at or near the hip. Instead of moving backward, it moves laterally toward the bar. During this very slight pause, the outside arm has moved behind the hips. At this point, both arms are brought forward and upward forcefully to time up with the free-swinging leg.

Biomechanical research has attempted to determine the value of upward force for each individual arm. This is done by measuring the maximum vertical velocity of each lever relative to the trunk during the liftoff phase. For almost all jumpers studied (Dapena, 1986), the arm farthest from the bar was the most active. This is probably because the outside arm correlates best with the action of the swinging leg. However, the inside arm can be made to generate additional force simply by getting it back behind the shoulder before leaving the ground.

High Jump Training Program

Workout samples for the high jump are shown in Figures 6.8 to 6.11. There is a sample weekly workout for the general preparation, specific preparation, power development, and competition mesocycles. These workouts are designed for college athletes involved in both indoor and outdoor seasons. Use the workouts as a general guide. Tailor your high jump training schedules to each individual athlete, taking into account factors such as weather, facilities, and especially your existing meet schedule.

General training activities are listed in the left column of each workout. Specific activities for each day of the week (which are taken directly from the left column) are listed in the right column. Each weekly workout includes running, and emphasis is placed on strength, technical, multithrow, flexibility, coordination, and psychological areas.

General Preparation Workout

1. **Easy jogging**
2. **Warm-up drills:**
   (a) High leg to 50
   (b) Fast legs to 50
   (c) Cariokas
   (d) A-B-Cs to 50
   (e) Stretching
3. **Skipping:**
   (a) Standard
   (b) Power
   (c) Double arms
4. **Stadium stairs:**
   (a) Sprinting up
   (b) Springing down
   (c) Hopping up
       (1) Single leg
       (2) Double legs
   (d) Hopping down
       (1) Single leg
       (2) Double legs
5. **Power runs:**
   (a) Hills
   (b) Belts
6. **Downhills:**
   (a) General
   (b) With takeoff
7. **Speed bounding:**
   (a) Single leg
   (b) Double legs
   (c) RR-LL
   (d) H-S-S-S-H
   (e) From 8 steps
8. **Power bounding:**
   (a) Single leg
   (b) Double legs
   (c) RR-LL
9. **Landing drills:**
   (a) Split
   (b) Alternate
   (c) Standing on knees
   (d) Full
10. **Penultimate step drills:**
    (a) 8 steps
    (b) 4 steps
11. **Hurdle hops:**
    (a) Flat
    (b) Box to 5 hurdles
    (c) Box to 8 hurdles
12. **Coach's mark to takeoff timing**
13. **Simulated runway:**
    (a) Full
    (b) 8 steps
    (c) 6 steps
14. **Weights:**
    (a) Special
        (1) Clean & jerk
        (2) Single-leg squats
        (3) Weighted vest
        (4) Lunges
    (b) Circuit
    (c) Power strength (general)
    (d) Arm drills
15. **Running sets:**
    (a) 40
    (b) 50
    (c) 60
    (d) 70
    (e) 80
    (f) 100
    (g) 110
    (h) 150
    (i) 180
    (j) 200
    (k) 300
    (l) 322
    (m) 400
    (n) 500
    (o) 550
    (p) 600
    (q) 800
    (r) 1,000
16. **Hurdles:** (same as above)
17. **Timed drop-downs:**
    (a) 20-30-20
    (b) 20-40-20
    (c) 20-50-20
    (d) 20-60

(continued)

Figure 6.8 Sample high jump workout during the general preparation mesocycle.

18. **Running drills:**
    (a) Backward
    (b) Circle
    (c) Figure 8
    (d) Side hills
    (e) Pop-ups
19. **Boxes:**
    (a) 14-16' bounding R-L-R-L;
        16-18' bounding R-L-R-L
    (b) RR-LL
    (c) Single leg through both legs
    (d) **HJ drills**
        (1) Table jumping
        (2) Ground-to-box-to-ground jumping
        (3) Ground-to-low-box jumping
    (e) **LJ drills**
        (1) Ground-to-box-to-ground jumping
        (2) Ground-to-low-box jumping
20. Meet with coach
21. **Films:**
    (a) Study session
    (b) To be filmed
22. Rehabilitation
23. Precompetition warm-up/check marks
24. Pool
25. **Medicine ball series:**
    (a) Double arms
    (b) Abdominal
26. Running circuit
27. Distance run

Legend of Work-to-Rest Ratios

Tuesday

(21a) (1 to 800) (stretch) (2 a-b-c-d × 6)
(8a to 100 on turf) (14 power)
(8a to 40 alternate)
(depth jumps × 8 over 8 hurdles)
(back 14 power – lateral bench hops)
(swimming)

Wednesday

(full warm-up) (technique session)
(approaches full – low jumps)
(15e on corner)
(cooldown)

Thursday

(1 to 2 mi) (stretch) (2 a-b-c-d × 5)
(17c × 6) (14 easy day power)
(heavy step-down 6" box) (6a × 6)
(lateral bench hops)
(heavy step-down)

Friday

Basketball
Stuffing & game

Saturday

Rest

Sunday

(14 full power cycle)

Monday

(1 to 800) (stretch) (technique session)
(10 constant jumps – no misses – then progress until 2 misses) (21)
(15k × 2) (15h × 4)
(cooldown)

Figure 6.8 *(continued)*

Specific Preparation Workout

1. **Easy jogging**
2. **Warm-up drills:**
   - (a) High leg to 50
   - (b) Fast legs to 50
   - (c) Cariokas
   - (d) A-B-Cs to 50
   - (e) Stretching
3. **Skipping:**
   - (a) Standard
   - (b) Power
   - (c) Double arms
4. **Stadium stairs:**
   - (a) Sprinting up
   - (b) Springing down
   - (c) Hopping up
     - (1) Single leg
     - (2) Double legs
   - (d) Hopping down
     - (1) Single leg
     - (2) Double legs
5. **Power runs:**
   - (a) Hills
   - (b) Belts
6. **Downhills:**
   - (a) General
   - (b) With takeoff
7. **Speed bounding:**
   - (a) Single leg
   - (b) Double legs
   - (c) RR-LL
   - (d) H-S-S-S-H
   - (e) From 8 steps
8. **Power bounding:**
   - (a) Single leg
   - (b) Double legs
   - (c) RR-LL
9. **Landing drills:**
   - (a) Split
   - (b) Alternate
   - (c) Standing on knees
   - (d) Full
10. **Penultimate step drills:**
    - (a) 8 steps
    - (b) 4 steps
11. **Hurdle hops:**
    - (a) Flat
    - (b) Box to 5 hurdles
    - (c) Box to 8 hurdles
12. Coach's mark to takeoff timing
13. **Simulated runway:**
    - (a) Full
    - (b) 8 steps
    - (c) 6 steps
14. **Weights:**
    - (a) Special
      - (1) Clean & jerk
      - (2) Single-leg squats
      - (3) Weighted vest
      - (4) Lunges
    - (b) Circuit
    - (c) Power strength (general)
    - (d) Arm drills
15. **Running sets:**
    - (a) 40
    - (b) 50
    - (c) 60
    - (d) 70
    - (e) 80
    - (f) 100
    - (g) 110
    - (h) 150
    - (i) 180
    - (j) 200
    - (k) 300
    - (l) 322
    - (m) 400
    - (n) 500
    - (o) 550
    - (p) 600
    - (q) 800
    - (r) 1,000
16. **Hurdles:** (same as above)
17. **Timed drop-downs:**
    - (a) 20-30-20
    - (b) 20-40-20
    - (c) 20-50-20
    - (d) 20-60

(continued)

Figure 6.9   Sample high jump workout during the specific preparation mesocycle.

18. **Running drills:**
    (a) Backward
    (b) Circle
    (c) Figure 8
    (d) Side hills
    (e) Pop-ups

19. **Boxes:**
    (a) 14-16' bounding R-L-R-L;
        16-18' bounding R-L-R-L
    (b) RR-LL
    (c) Single leg through both legs
    (d) **HJ drills**
        (1) Table jumping
        (2) Ground-to-box-to-ground jumping
        (3) Ground-to-low-box jumping
    (e) **LJ drills**
        (1) Ground-to-box-to-ground jumping
        (2) Ground-to-low-box jumping

20. Meet with coach

21 **Films:**
    (a) Study session
    (b) To be filmed

22. Rehabilitation

23. Precompetition warm-up/check marks

24. Pool

25. **Medicine ball series:**
    (a) Double arms
    (b) Abdominal

26. Running circuit

27. Distance run

Legend of Work-to-Rest Ratios

Monday

(1 × 800) (stretch) (2 a-b-c-d × 5 ea.)
(jump session) (moderate height × 14)
(at competition move bar up until 2 misses)
(15k × 2) (15h × 4) (8c × 14 ground contacts)
(3a × 200) (cooldown)

Tuesday

(1 to 1,200) (stretch) (2 a-b-c-d × 4 ea.)
(17c × 6 drop-downs) (10b × 20)
(15e on corner)
(14a)

Wednesday

(1 × 1,200) (stretch) (drills as you feel)
(15k × 3)
(3c × 14 to 40)

Thursday

(1 × 800) (stretch) (2 a-b-c-d × 6)
(outside to turf – 8a × 40 to 80)
(8c × 20 ground contacts × 5)
(14a)

Friday

(1 to 2 mi) (stretch)
(5a to 200 × 6 drop-downs)

Saturday

Rest

Sunday

(14a)

Figure 6.9   *(continued)*

Power Development Workout

1. **Easy jogging**
2. **Warm-up drills:**
   - (a) High leg to 50
   - (b) Fast legs to 50
   - (c) Cariokas
   - (d) A-B-Cs to 50
   - (e) Stretching
3. **Skipping:**
   - (a) Standard
   - (b) Power
   - (c) Double arms
4. **Stadium stairs:**
   - (a) Sprinting up
   - (b) Springing down
   - (c) Hopping up
     - (1) Single leg
     - (2) Double legs
   - (d) Hopping down
     - (1) Single leg
     - (2) Double legs
5. **Power runs:**
   - (a) Hills
   - (b) Belts
6. **Downhills:**
   - (a) General
   - (b) With takeoff
7. **Speed bounding:**
   - (a) Single leg
   - (b) Double legs
   - (c) RR-LL
   - (d) H-S-S-S-H
   - (e) From 8 steps
8. **Power bounding:**
   - (a) Single leg
   - (b) Double legs
   - (c) RR-LL
9. **Landing drills:**
   - (a) Split
   - (b) Alternate
   - (c) Standing on knees
   - (d) Full
10. **Penultimate step drills:**
    - (a) 8 steps
    - (b) 4 steps
11. **Hurdle hops:**
    - (a) Flat
    - (b) Box to 5 hurdles
    - (c) Box to 8 hurdles
12. Coach's mark to takeoff timing
13. **Simulated runway:**
    - (a) Full
    - (b) 8 steps
    - (c) 6 steps
14. **Weights:**
    - (a) Special
      - (1) Clean & jerk
      - (2) Single-leg squats
      - (3) Weighted vest
      - (4) Lunges
    - (b) Circuit
    - (c) Power strength (general)
    - (d) Arm drills
15. **Running sets:**
    - (a) 40
    - (b) 50
    - (c) 60
    - (d) 70
    - (e) 80
    - (f) 100
    - (g) 110
    - (h) 150
    - (i) 180
    - (j) 200
    - (k) 300
    - (l) 322
    - (m) 400
    - (n) 500
    - (o) 550
    - (p) 600
    - (q) 800
    - (r) 1,000
16. **Hurdles:** (same as above)
17. **Timed drop-downs:**
    - (a) 20-30-20
    - (b) 20-40-20
    - (c) 20-50-20
    - (d) 20-60

(continued)

Figure 6.10   Sample high jump workout during the power development mesocycle.

18. **Running drills:**
    (a) Backward
    (b) Circle
    (c) Figure 8
    (d) Side hills
    (e) Pop-ups

19. **Boxes:**
    (a) 14-16' bounding R-L-R-L;
        16-18' bounding R-L-R-L
    (b) RR-LL
    (c) Single leg through both legs
    (d) **HJ drills**
        (1) Table jumping
        (2) Ground-to-box-to-ground jumping
        (3) Ground-to-low-box jumping
    (e) **LJ drills**
        (1) Ground-to-box-to-ground jumping
        (2) Ground-to-low-box jumping

20. Meet with coach

21 **Films:**
    (a) Study session
    (b) To be filmed

22. Rehabilitation

23. Precompetition warm-up/check marks

24. Pool

25. **Medicine ball series:**
    (a) Double arms
    (b) Abdominal

26. Running circuit

27. Distance run

Legend of Work-to-Rest Ratios

Monday

(1 easy) (stretch) (2a-b-c-d × 4 ea.)
(jump session – approaches low jump)
(15e × 4 on curve) (4a × 4) (3c × 6 to 80)
(8c to 18 ground contacts) (4a × 3)
(6b to 6) (cooldown)

Tuesday

(1 to 800) (stretch) (2a-b-c-d × 4 to 30)
(17d not timed × 5) (7c × 3 ea. leg)
(14c power – ½ squats – ½ squats)
(8a × 4 to 14 ground contacts alternate)
(leg press – leg press – 8c × 4 to 14 g.c.)
(cleans-cleans-box to floor over hurdle × 8)
(finish weights on P cycle) (cooldown)

Wednesday

(warm-up) (13 approaches only)
(to swimming pool)

Thursday

(1 to 2 mi) (stretch) (2a-b-c-d × 4 to 40)
(6b × 12) (5b to 20 strides)
(14c power cycle – day 2)
(7d × 6) (cooldown)

Friday

(easy run to hill)
(6a × 4 drop-downs) (cooldown)

Saturday

Rest

Sunday

(1 to 800) (stretch) (17d × 5 not timed)
(14 power cycle – day 3)
(general repeat of Tuesday)

Figure 6.10   *(continued)*

Competition Workout

1. **Easy jogging**
2. **Warm-up drills:**
   (a) High leg to 50
   (b) Fast legs to 50
   (c) Cariokas
   (d) A-B-Cs to 50
   (e) Stretching
3. **Skipping:**
   (a) Standard
   (b) Power
   (c) Double arms
4. **Stadium stairs:**
   (a) Sprinting up
   (b) Springing down
   (c) Hopping up
      (1) Single leg
      (2) Double legs
   (d) Hopping down
      (1) Single leg
      (2) Double legs
5. **Power runs:**
   (a) Hills
   (b) Belts
6. **Downhills:**
   (a) General
   (b) With takeoff
7. **Speed bounding:**
   (a) Single leg
   (b) Double legs
   (c) RR-LL
   (d) H-S-S-S-H
   (e) From 8 steps
8. **Power bounding:**
   (a) Single leg
   (b) Double legs
   (c) RR-LL
9. **Landing drills:**
   (a) Split
   (b) Alternate
   (c) Standing on knees
   (d) Full
10. **Penultimate step drills:**
    (a) 8 steps
    (b) 4 steps

11. **Hurdle hops:**
    (a) Flat
    (b) Box to 5 hurdles
    (c) Box to 8 hurdles
12. **Coach's mark to takeoff timing**
13. **Simulated runway:**
    (a) Full
    (b) 8 steps
    (c) 6 steps
14. **Weights:**
    (a) Special
       (1) Clean & jerk
       (2) Single-leg squats
       (3) Weighted vest
       (4) Lunges
    (b) Circuit
    (c) Power strength (general)
    (d) Arm drills
15. **Running sets:**
    (a) 40
    (b) 50
    (c) 60
    (d) 70
    (e) 80
    (f) 100
    (g) 110
    (h) 150
    (i) 180
    (j) 200
    (k) 300
    (l) 322
    (m) 400
    (n) 500
    (o) 550
    (p) 600
    (q) 800
    (r) 1,000
16. **Hurdles:** (same as above)
17. **Timed drop-downs:**
    (a) 20-30-20
    (b) 20-40-20
    (c) 20-50-20
    (d) 20-60

(continued)

Figure 6.11 Sample high jump workout during the competition mesocycle.

18. **Running drills:**
    (a) Backward
    (b) Circle
    (c) Figure 8
    (d) Side hills
    (e) Pop-ups

19. **Boxes:**
    (a) 14-16' bounding R-L-R-L;
        16-18' bounding R-L-R-L
    (b) RR-LL
    (c) Single leg through both legs
    (d) **HJ drills**
        (1) Table jumping
        (2) Ground-to-box-to-ground jumping
        (3) Ground-to-low-box jumping
    (e) **LJ drills**
        (1) Ground-to-box-to-ground jumping
        (2) Ground-to-low-box jumping

20. Meet with coach

21 **Films:**
    (a) Study session
    (b) To be filmed

22. Rehabilitation

23. Precompetition warm-up/check marks

24. Pool

25. **Medicine ball series:**
    (a) Double arms
    (b) Abdominal

26. Running circuit

27. Distance run

Legend of Work-to-Rest Ratios

Monday

(1 to 800) (stretch) (2 a-b-c-d × 5)
(light jump session for confidence)
(17a × 5) (ladder drills with takeoff)
(7c × 5) (7a on stadium stairs)
(4a × 3 – best of year)

Tuesday

(light warm-up) (stretch)
(17b × 6)
(18b with simulated takeoff)
(15h × 4)
(no lifting)

Wednesday

(light warm-up – drills as you feel)

Thursday

(light warm-up – drills as you feel)
(17a × 4)

Friday

Rest

Saturday

Competition (conference championships)

Sunday

Rest

Figure 6.11   *(continued)*

Chapter 7
Pole Vault

Bob Fraley ▪ Doug Fraley

The pole vault is one of the most analyzed athletic activities. It is also one of the most exciting events to watch. In the last decade, with the increase in television coverage, the pole vault has become a popular subject for commercial advertising. But the vault is more than an event to be analyzed or commercialized. It is an event that inspires great emotion and much tradition.

Keys to Pole Vaulting

- Achieve maximum velocity without disturbing the vaulter-pole system.
- During the left support stride phase, having the left hand in front of the chest with the wrist above the elbow prevents taking off under.
- Before the tip of the pole touches the back of the plant box extend both arms to their maximum height.
- At takeoff, the top hand should be perpendicular to the toe of the takeoff foot. Any variation inside or outside will result in loss of velocity and angle.
- Success during the swing is determined by the vaulter's success in each of the prior phases of the vault.
- To line up with the pole, start the turn before completion of the extension.

Coach's Tip

The biggest improvement in the vault will come from improving the mechanics of the approach and from improvements in physical training.

Athletes who have competed in the pole vault remain loyal to the event. They know it takes a pioneer spirit to be a vaulter, and they know success does not come overnight. Vaulting is one of the few events in sports where it is acceptable for competitors to assist each other by checking the six-stride mark, catching each other's takeoff point, or actually filming each other during competition. Vaulters know that when the names are called, some of them may feel the wind at their backs and others may find it blowing in their faces, but the same results are expected of all. The former vaulter sitting in the stands knows what's happening on the field. He or she has been there, has felt the bend of the pole, experienced the mighty launch skyward when the pole releases its energy, and knows the thrill of flying over the bar and heading for the cushion far below. Vaulting is both challenging and frustrating, and it requires years of work as well as a change in technique.

There are eleven important components of the pole vault program: strength, power, speed, endurance, flexibility, technique, orientation, coordination, recovery, mental preparation, and diet. The technical component made up of the approach, pole plant, takeoff, swing-up, extension, and turn will be the focus of this chapter. However, too many coaches and athletes concentrate only on the technical component of the vault and fail to recognize the major role played by the other ten components in the overall development and success of the vaulter. Coaches will be surprised how quickly technique improves as the vaulter improves his or her strength, power, speed, and coordination.

To have a high grip on the pole, the vaulter must have a good takeoff; to move a pole 30 pounds heavier than body weight, the vaulter must have a good takeoff; and to have a good takeoff, the vaulter must generate power and speed in the run-up. Successful vaulting requires hours of conditioning, strength, power, and speed work developed through an event-specific training program. This program must teach the vaulter the proper setup of each phase of the approach to synchronize acceleration, the lowering of the pole, the plant mechanics, and the takeoff that gives the vaulter the best possible angle and velocity to stay free of any breaking forces. These skills take years of training to develop. One only need look at Sergey Bubka to recognize that he possesses great power and speed that allow him to grip the pole at 16 feet 8 inches and to jump on a pole rated at 10.8 flex and vault higher than 20 feet. Today an athlete like Bubka is the exception, not the rule, but he is the model for all vaulters because he has what it takes to propel him to all-time heights.

Coach's Tip

In situations where the vaulter may need to use a lighter pole, it is strongly recommended the grip be lowered and a shorter pole be used at or above the vaulter's body weight.

The technical model presented in this chapter applies to a right-handed vaulter. In this model, the right hand is the top hand, the left hand the lower hand, and the left foot is the takeoff foot.

In the vaulter-pole system, vaulter and pole act as a single unit. The pole is carried at an angle so that the shoulders, back, and hips stay in line. This allows the athlete to use good sprint mechanics, develop rhythm, lower the pole, and execute the plant without losing posture and velocity. The vaulter must be careful not to make a sudden movement with any part of the body that will affect the angle and weight of the pole, destroying the balance between vaulter and pole and creating a timing and space problem.

Safety

The coach must be alert to dangerous situations and circumstances and be ready to take action to prevent injury to the athlete. The coach needs to provide the following duties:

- Proper instruction
- Proper progression of skills
- Warning of the inherent dangers in the event
- Warning of the dangers caused by using improper technique
- Adequate supervision
- Safe equipment
- Maintenance of equipment
- Enforcing the rules of the event
- Developing and keeping on file a written training program
- Developing in the vaulters an attitude and responsibility for safety

Approach

In the past, there has been much emphasis on building maximum speed while coming down the runway. Although speed is a crucial component in the success of the vault, the approach run must consist of much more than just raw speed. The fact that the vaulter is carrying a long weighted object requires a different sprinting rhythm than that of a sprinter or long jumper. Mistakes made during any phase of the approach will be difficult to correct and will have a negative effect on the entire vault.

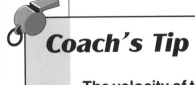

Coach's Tip

The velocity of the vaulter between 10 meters to 5 meters from the plant box is a key indicator of the vaulter's potential.

The goal of the approach is to reach the plant and takeoff positions at a maximum controlled velocity. The vaulter must be able to coordinate the stride pattern with the lowering of the pole, being careful not to create a negative effect on the vaulter-pole system while trying to achieve the approach velocity necessary for a good competitive height.

Studies conducted by Dr. Peter McGinnis (1991a), through the USA Track and Field Scientific Services program, on horizontal velocity from 10 to 5 meters from the box show the estimated minimum velocity required for the following heights: 5.50 meters (18 feet 1/2 inch) is 8.7 meters per second; 5.80 meters (19 feet 1/4 inch) is 9.1 meters per second. Studies show the approach run velocity of Sergey Bubka to be between 9.6 and 9.9 meters per second. Velocities of selected elite vaulters from various competitions are listed in Tables 7.1 to 7.4. In studies conducted by Tony Feroah at the 1992 Pole Vault Summit in Reno, Nevada,

Coach's Tip

The best way to eliminate potential mistakes is to find an optimal body position and pole angle before taking the first stride.

Table 7.1
Velocities of Selected Vaulters at the 1987 IAAF World Championship

	Crossbar height (m)	Velocity 15-10 m from box		Velocity 10-5 m from box		Result (0 - make, x = miss)
		(m/s)	(ft/s)	(m/s)	(ft/s)	
Sergey Bubka	5.70	9.42	(30.91)	9.65	(31.66)	0
	5.85	9.47	(31.07)	9.77	(32.05)	0
	6.05	9.42	(30.91)	9.67	(31.73)	x
		9.42	(30.91)	9.65	(31.66)	x
Thierry Vigneron	5.50	9.16	(30.05)	9.14	(29.99)	0
	5.70	9.56	(31.36)	9.43	(30.95)	0
	5.80	9.42	(30.91)	9.40	(30.84)	x
		9.42	(30.91)	9.43	(30.95)	0
	5.85	9.47	(31.07)	9.36	(30.71)	x
		9.45	(31.00)	9.42	(30.91)	x
		9.42	(30.91)	9.33	(30.61)	x
Rodion Gataullin	5.60	9.42	(30.91)	9.52	(31.23)	0
	5.70	9.31	(30.54)	9.09	(29.83)	x
		9.42	(30.91)	9.54	(31.30)	0
	5.80	9.35	(30.68)	9.60	(31.50)	x
		9.40	(30.84)	9.60	(31.50)	0
	5.85	9.40	(30.84)	9.67	(31.73)	x
		9.36	(30.71)	9.54	(31.30)	x
		9.26	(30.38)	9.33	(30.61)	x

Note. Used with permission of Dr. Peter McGinnis.

on high school vaulters (14 feet 6 inches to 16 feet), the velocities ranged from 7.9 to 8.7 meters per second.

At the end of the run, the vaulter must not only be moving at great speed but have energy, rhythm, posture, and power to execute a proper plant and a powerful takeoff.

The vaulter must position the feet so that the center of mass remains high as he or she takes the first step and so that vaulter and pole do not separate. Stepping back and forth with long strides can negatively affect the posture of the vaulter.

First Stride

To set up for the first stride, the vaulter lifts the pole to about 80° to make it as light as possible. The weight of the pole should be on the body and right hand, which is held just in front of the right hip. The vaulter then takes a short step backward (about 15 inches), allowing the shoulders to move back and set the pole angle, then steps forward, allowing the shoulders to line up with the hips. This movement creates the vaulter-pole system (Figure 7.1a). Starting down the runway out of position will adversely affect the vaulter's posture, the lowering of the pole, the plant mechanics, and the takeoff.

In the first two to three strides, the vaulter must drive powerfully off the mark, taking care to maintain optimal body posture and pole position (Figure 7.1b). To do this, the pole is pushed in front of the body to prevent the right hand from drifting back behind the right hip.

The approach is a series of setups that lead to the takeoff. In the first 8 to 10 strides (depending on the number of strides in the approach), the vaulter is building speed, with

Table 7.2
Velocities of Selected Vaulters at the 1988 Olympics

	Crossbar height (m)	Velocity 15-10 m from box (m/s)	(ft/s)	Velocity 10-5 m from box (m/s)	(ft/s)	Result (0 - make, x = miss)
Grigoriy Yegorov	5.50	9.23	(30.28)	9.21	(30.22)	0
	5.70	9.29	(30.47)	9.26	(30.38)	x
		9.28	(30.45)	9.09	(29.83)	0
	5.80	9.36	(30.71)	9.42	(30.91)	0
	5.90	9.14	(29.99)	8.93	(29.30)	x
		9.16	(30.05)	8.77	(28.77)	x
		9.09	(29.83)	8.77	(28.77)	x
Earl Bell	5.40	8.88	(29.13)	9.21	(30.22)	0
	5.70	8.87	(29.10)	9.23	(30.28)	0
	5.75	8.87	(29.10)	9.11	(29.89)	x
		8.87	(29.10)	9.16	(30.05)	x
		9.01	(29.56)	9.07	(29.76)	x
Kory Tarpenning	5.50	8.80	(28.87)	9.04	(29.66)	0
	5.65	8.87	(29.10)	7.76	(25.46)	x
		8.88	(29.13)	9.12	(29.92)	x
		8.95	(29.36)	9.17	(30.08)	x

Note. Used with permission of Dr. Peter McGinnis.

the cadence of each stride faster than the one before it. This gradual acceleration is synchronized so that the vaulter's body posture does not change (Figures 7.1c-d).

Pole Drop

If done correctly, the first 8 to 10 strides of the run will set the vaulter up for a rapid

Figure 7.1   The pole vault approach.

Table 7.3
Velocities of Selected Vaulters at the 1989-1990 TAC Championship

	Crossbar height (m)	Velocity 15-10 m from box (m/s)	(ft/s)	Velocity 10-5 m from box (m/s)	(ft/s)	Result (0 - make, x = miss)
Doug Fraley	5.59	8.93	(29.29)	9.26	(30.38)	0
	5.69	9.09	(29.83)	9.09	(29.83)	0
	5.79	9.09	(29.83)	9.26	(30.38)	x
		8.93	(29.29)	9.43	(30.95)	x
		8.93	(29.29)	9.26	(30.38)	x
Dean Starkey	5.39	9.26	(30.38)	9.43	(30.95)	0
	5.49	9.26	(30.38)	9.26	(30.38)	x
		9.09	(29.83)	9.26	(30.38)	0
	5.59	8.93	(29.29)	9.26	(30.38)	x
		9.26	(30.38)	9.26	(30.38)	0
	5.69	9.26	(30.38)	9.43	(30.95)	x
		9.26	(30.38)	9.43	(30.95)	0
	5.79	8.93	(29.29)	9.80	(32.17)	x
		8.93	(29.29)	9.43	(30.95)	x
		8.93	(29.29)	9.62	(31.54)	x
Earl Bell	5.34	8.55	(28.05)	9.00	(29.52)	0
	5.58	8.85	(29.03)	9.26	(30.38)	0
	5.66	8.77	(28.77)	9.28	(30.45)	0
	5.74	8.77	(28.77)	9.35	(30.68)	x
		8.77	(28.77)	9.35	(30.68)	x
		8.85	(29.03)	9.26	(30.38)	0
	5.81	8.77	(28.77)	9.28	(30.45)	x
		8.85	(29.03)	9.28	(30.45)	x
Tim Bright	5.50	9.01	(29.56)	9.52	(31.23)	0
	5.66	8.93	(29.30)	9.68	(31.76)	x
		9.17	(30.09)	9.35	(30.68)	0
	5.74	9.01	(29.56)	9.28	(30.45)	x
		9.17	(30.09)	9.26	(30.38)	x (run-through)
Kory Tarpenning	5.50	9.10	(29.86)	9.57	(31.40)	0
	5.66	9.17	(30.09)	9.43	(30.94)	x
		9.01	(29.56)	9.43	(30.94)	x
	5.74	9.01	(29.56)	9.57	(31.40)	x

Note. Used with permission of Dr. Peter McGinnis.

Table 7.4
Velocities of Selected Vaulters at the 1990 Goodwill Games

	Crossbar height (m)	Velocity 15-10 m from box		Velocity 10-5 m from box		Result (0 - make, x = miss)
		(m/s)	(ft/s)	(m/s)	(ft/s)	
Maksim Tarasov	5.57	9.71	(31.85)	9.35	(30.66)	0
	5.77	9.80	(32.17)	9.43	(30.95)	x
		9.71	(31.85)	9.43	(30.95)	x
		9.71	(31.85)	9.43	(30.95)	x
Igor Potapovich	5.57	9.35	(30.66)	9.62	(31.55)	x
		9.52	(31.25)	9.26	(30.38)	x
		9.35	(30.66)	9.35	(30.66)	0
	5.77	9.43	(30.95)	9.26	(30.38)	x
		9.52	(31.25)	9.09	(29.83)	x
		9.52	(31.25)	9.43	(30.95)	x
Earl Bell	5.37	8.85	(29.04)	9.09	(29.83)	0
	5.57	9.09	(29.83)	9.09	(29.83)	x
		9.09	(29.83)	9.17	(30.10)	x
		9.09	(29.83)	9.17	(30.10)	x
Rodion Gataullin	5.72	9.71	(31.85)	9.52	(31.25)	0
	5.82	9.62	(31.55)	9.43	(30.95)	0
	5.92	9.71	(31.85)	9.35	(30.66)	x
		9.71	(31.85)	9.52	(31.25)	0
	6.08	9.52	(31.25)	9.35	(30.66)	x
		9.52	(31.25)	9.52	(31.25)	x
		9.43	(30.95)	9.52	(31.25)	x
Grigoriy Yegorov	5.57	9.35	(30.66)	9.52	(31.23)	0
	5.72	9.52	(31.23)	9.43	(30.95)	0
	5.82	9.52	(31.23)	9.52	(31.23)	x
		9.43	(30.95)	9.43	(30.95)	x
		9.52	(31.23)	9.52	(31.23)	0
	5.87	9.71	(31.85)	9.52	(31.23)	x
		9.52	(31.23)	9.52	(31.23)	0
	5.92	9.71	(31.85)	9.17	(30.10)	x (run-through)

Note. Used with permission of Dr. Peter McGinnis.

Andrzej Krzesinski's Technique

The plant, takeoff, swing-up, extension, turn, and bar clearance developed by Andrzej

Krzesinski are shown below.

Note. Used with permission of Andrzej Krzesinski.

lowering of the pole. Having good posture and having the pole at an angle of 65° to 70° is crucial to the success of the next 7 to 8 strides and the takeoff.

As the pole drops, the strides accelerate, and the key is to time the lowering of the pole so that it arrives near the horizontal position when the vaulter is on the left support phase of the third to last stride before takeoff (Figure 7.1d-f). If the pole drop is timed correctly, the stride cadence will quicken similar to being pulled by a supramaximum sprint device.

With correct timing of the pole drop, the vaulter never has to deal with the weight of the pole and will maintain good posture without loss of momentum and position at takeoff (Figure 7.1g).

Pole Plant

Traditionally, the takeoff point for many American vaulters has been approximately 6 to 14 inches inside the optimum takeoff point. A primary reason for this is that many of the top vaulters used a plant technique in which the vaulter lowered the pole with the left hand, straightened and drew back the right elbow, locked the pole into a horizontal position for several strides, and extended the left arm straight out between the third and second to last strides before takeoff. As a result of these mechanical actions, the right shoulder opened up, causing the vaulter to lean back and producing a long stride that resulted in poor posture (step under and hips out of position) at takeoff. The pole bent before the vaulter rolled up on the toe of the takeoff foot, resulting in loss of power and failure to achieve full body extension and a high plant.

The plant mechanics begin at the back of the runway with a series of setups. The starting position sets up the rhythm of the run for the first 8 to 10 strides. The rhythm of the run sets up the lowering of the pole for the next 3 to 5 strides, and the lowering of the pole sets up good body posture for the plant, which takes place during the last 3 strides. The plant mechanics set up the takeoff, which determines the style of swing technique the vaulter will use.

Figure 7.2   Mechanics of the plant.

Coach's Tip

The timing of the lowering of the pole and lever action of the right elbow put the vaulter into the correct body position to execute the proper mechanics from the third to the last stride through the takeoff.

To understand the proper mechanics of the plant, think of the left hand as a fulcrum and the right arm as a lever. The left hand is held at chest level and under the pole, and the wrist never drops below the left elbow. The lowering of the pole is determined by the bending of the right elbow.

Transition From Horizontal to Vertical

When the vaulter is on the left stride support phase (see Figure 7.2a), the pole is nearly horizontal to the runway with the right hand close to the hip, the right elbow bent, and the upper right arm in line with the shoulder. The left hand is in front of the chest with the wrist above the elbow.

During the transition between the left and right strides (Figure 7.2b), both hands roll over, with the right hand moving to shoulder level. The left arm is located in front of the chest with the elbow placed under the pole without extending the forearm toward the box.

As the vaulter moves into the right support phase, the right hand moves to head level in front of the forehead with the right elbow bent and turned out. The left hand is in front of the face with the left wrist and elbow under the pole.

As the vaulter moves forward off the right foot and onto the left, he or she must synchro-

nize the action of the right arm with that of the left leg. Both arms are pushed up, and at the moment the takeoff foot is planted, the right hand should be at its highest point over the takeoff point (Figure 7.2c)

Takeoff

If we have learned anything from coaches and athletes from the former Soviet Union, it is that the takeoff point is critical to the success of the vault. A free takeoff with both the right and left hands extended to their highest point when the takeoff foot is up on the toe and the pole is coming into contact with the back of the box will result in a fast, free, and uninterrupted takeoff. The takeoff will determine the vault style as well as pole speed, size, and grip.

During the past two decades, many elite American vaulters have been taking off under, and for years coaches have argued about whether or not the left arm should be straight and whether or not it applies force at takeoff. In most situations, vaulters who have traditionally been under on the takeoff have used a straight left arm to keep the pole away from the body.

When synchronized, the correct rhythm of approach, lowering of the pole, and plant mechanics produce a proper body position, allowing the takeoff foot to be brought out to the correct takeoff point with both arms fully

Coach's Tip

At the 1994 USA Track and Field Pole Vault Summit, Vataly Petrov stressed the importance of the vaulter thinking "arms first, then feet" as he or she moves from the right stride to the left takeoff foot.

Nicole Rieger

This is an illustration of Nicole Rieger's 3.9-meter (12-foot 9-1/2-inch) vault effort at a European developmental roots in Europe and Asia and is now recognized by the International Amateur pion, Melissa Price, at the 1994 USA Track and Field Championships.

competition. Her velocity was 7.35 meters per second. The women's pole vault had its Athletic Federation (IAAF). The United States recently crowned its first female cham-

Note. Used with permission of Dr. Horst Adamczewski.

extended (Figure 7.2c) and with no need for the athlete to force the bottom arm. The top hand will be perpendicular to the toe of the takeoff foot. Any variation inside or outside will result in loss of velocity and angle at takeoff.

As the vaulter moves over his or her takeoff foot, if the pole begins to bend while the foot is flat on the ground, the vault is under. The vaulter who takes off at the correct point will be high up on the toe of the takeoff foot and leaving the ground when the pole starts bending.

The goal is to have an uninterrupted free takeoff so that the vaulter takes off with the pole rather than against it. In studying elite vaulters, you will see that some accomplish this by allowing the left elbow to bend and others use a straight left arm through the drive

off the takeoff foot. A common characteristic of successful vaults using both techniques is the time it takes the vaulter to rotate back to align the head with the right arm in the early phase of the swing.

Swing

Some vaulters drop the lead knee into a double-leg swing (Figure 7.3a) and others keep the lead knee up and the takeoff leg back in a long position (Figure 7.3b).

Which style is used is not as important as what takes place in the next sequence. The vaulter will either continue with an extended left leg, allowing it to swing straight through to the inverted position (Figure 7.4a), or will swing back into a tuck position, which changes the loading of the pole (Figure 7.4b).

With the straight leg technique, the vaulter will continue to load the pole and, in the later stages of the extension, will be positioned such that the pole will actually push him or her through the extension and turn. In contrast, film analysis shows that with the tuck style, as the vaulter brings both knees in, the top of the pole does not stay bent. Instead, the pole releases to a vertical position (Figure 7.4b), resulting in energy loss, with the vaulter being pulled and having to compensate with a strong extension as the pole rotation nears the vertical position.

Extension and Turn

By now, the vaulter has put the energy into the pole and is ready to get into position to receive it back in the form of vertical lift over the crossbar. To put the extension and turn in simple terms, think of the pole as a bow and the vaulter as an arrow. The goal is to have the arrow pointed in the right direction before the bow releases. How the body lines up with the pole is dependent on the amount of rotation gained during the swing.

If the vaulter has swung to the optimal position (Figure 7.5a, p. 128), the hips will

Figure 7.3   The swing.

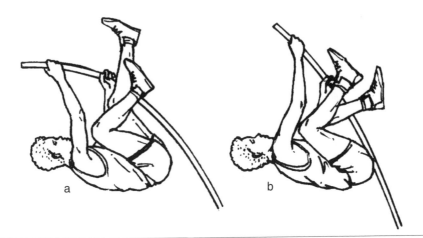

Figure 7.4   The swing: (a) inverted position; (b) tuck position.

be higher than the shoulders and the legs will be in a nearly straight position against the pole with the heels of the feet pointing skyward. From this position, the extension and turn are very simple and partially simultaneous. The hips and shoulder must now trade places, and the body will unfold as this happens. As the extension unfolds, the vaulter will begin to feel the weight on his or her hands. This is a good sign because

it means that the pole has remained bent until the vaulter is in position to rise with it with little or no energy loss.

At the midpoint of the extension or unfolding, it is crucial that the vaulter begin to turn. Often a vaulter will get completely extended, back to the bar, before initiating the turn, so he or she must try to turn after the thrust of the pole. This results in the vaulter turning on a straight pole, which causes the body to fade toward the bar. If the turn is timed to occur between the midpoint and last part of the extension, this allows the right hand and right hip to join, and the shoulders will drop in line with the pole, creating the arrow effect. The vaulter can now rise with his or her belly to the bar with no energy being wasted.

Another common mistake made in this phase of the vault is dropping the left foot out at the bar when initiating the turn. The left foot must act as a post, with the rest of the body rotating around it (Figure 7.5b, p. 128). This helps the vaulter stay in line with the pole while being pushed upward and does not diminish the vertical energy returned by the pole.

As discussed in the swing section, if the vaulter hasn't rotated back far enough and the hips are low and the shoulders high, a

Doug Fraley

The tuck style of vaulting is shown in this analysis of Doug Fraley's 5.40-meter (17-foot 8-1/2-inch) vault at the 1988 Modesto competition. This style is characterized by both knees being brought in toward the chest in the later stages of the swing-up.

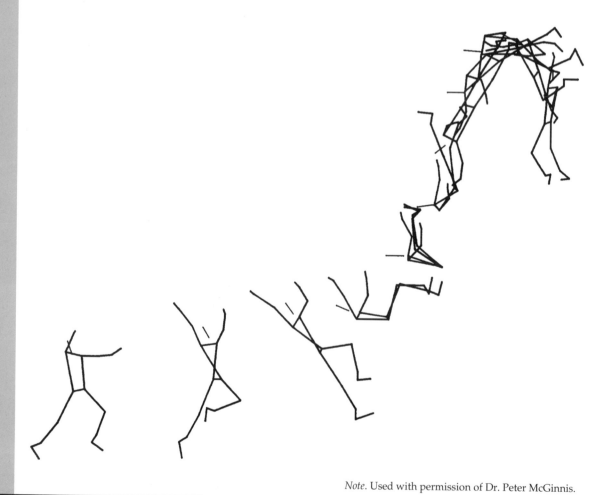

Note. Used with permission of Dr. Peter McGinnis.

different style of extension will be necessary. From this tuck or "bucket" position (Figure 7.4b), the vaulter will have a pole that is already beginning to unbend. While the pole is "running away," the vaulter must use the "shoot" extension to catch up with the pole and capture the vertical energy. This maneuver must be very forceful so that the vaulter can get lined up with the pole again. The rules for the turn phase of the shoot are the same as those for the turn in the straight-leg swing. As the vaulter is shooting up the pole, he or she must turn early to ensure proper alignment.

Although the "tuck and shoot" is not as efficient as the straight-leg swing, numerous 18-foot-plus vaulters have become very proficient at it and have had great success worldwide. The majority of vaulters fall somewhere between the two styles.

Mike Tully

The straight-leg style of vaulting is shown in this analysis of Mike Tully's 5.87-meter (19-foot 3-inch) vault at the 1988 Modesto competition. Although this style is referred to as the straight-leg technique, observers may see a slight flexion in the left leg as it swings past the right leg in the later stages of the swing-up.

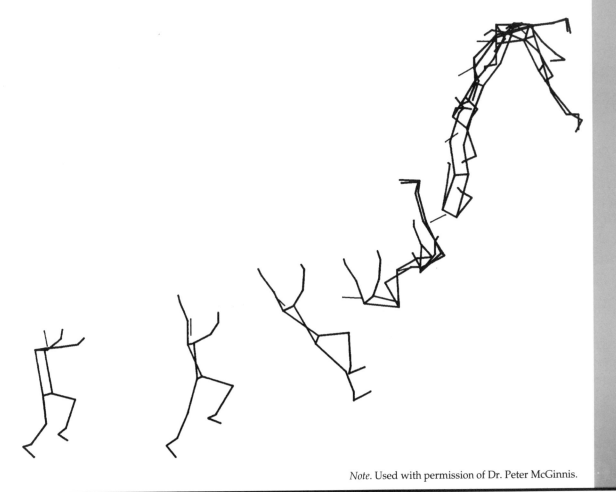

Note. Used with permission of Dr. Peter McGinnis.

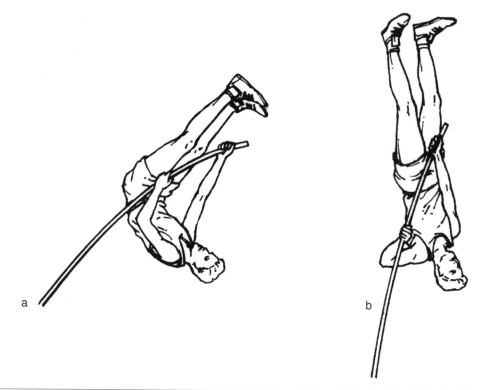

a

b

Figure 7.5   The extension.

Training Principles for the Pole Vault

The following are training principles we use to develop our annual program. Many of the principles may seem general in nature but are based on studies by Tudor Bompa and concepts developed by Andrzej Krzesinski and Vataly Petrov.

Principle 1: Active Participation

Depending on the age and experience of the athlete, the coach may want to sit down with the pole vaulter to discuss his or her progress. The young, developing vaulter will most likely depend solely on the coach for planning, whereas the experienced vaulter may want to have input into the workout plan. Generally, the more experienced the vaulter, the more input he or she is likely to have. One thing the coach must always consider is that personal problems (e.g., relationships, school, jobs) can have an impact on athletic performance.

Principle 2: Start With a Broad-Based Program

In discussing training principles for pole vaulters at the USA Track and Field Clinic in Fresno,

Coach's Tip

To simplify the turn, the vaulter brings the right hand to the right hip as he or she swings up. This results in the vaulter making a quarter turn on the pole early, preventing a late turn in the extension and turn phase of the vault.

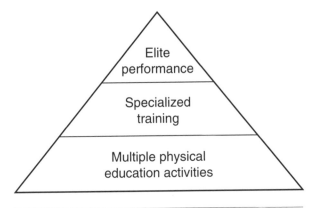

Figure 7.6 Broad-based program for pole vault development.

Andrzej Krzesinski (1993), the former national coach in Poland, presented a plan that has been in use in Eastern Europe for many years. The plan uses a broad foundation of physical education activities to develop the motor skills and physical fitness to build specific athletic skills (see Figure 7.6). As the athlete ages and develops all-around skills, he or she gradually moves to more specialized training.

Principle 3: Specialization

Studies by exercise physiologists have shown that the body adapts to the activity it is exposed to the most. Applying this principle to the pole vault, the vaulter needs to develop a series of drills that are designed to simulate specific phases of the vault and continue to rehearse each drill. In our experience, it is best for the vaulter to work on a specific drill for a few repetitions, rest, then come back and repeat the drills.

Principle 4: Individualization

In developing an annual training program, the coach must keep in mind four factors: (1) age of the athlete, (2) physical maturity, (3) mental maturity, and (4) athletic experience. Based on these factors, the coach must develop a program that challenges the athlete but does not push the individual too far. After years of working with athletes, experience has taught us that even though athletes can compete at the same level as their teammates in a meet, some may not be capable of working at the same level in practice.

Principle 5: Progressive Increase

Some important questions facing the coach and athlete are: How fast to progress? How much (or how little) work? How many vaults? How much recovery time? How much weight? How many drills? The progressive load principle answers these questions but with some modifications. Coaches and athletes know that the training load must be increased gradually depending on the vaulter's physical and mental abilities to handle the increase. But what is the best way to increase the load so that the athlete continues to improve? There are two methods widely used by coaches. One is a steady increase in the volume of work (Figure 7.7), and the other is a step method (Figure 7.8).

Studies done in Russia and Germany have had a major impact on planning the annual training program (Bompa, 1990). These studies have shown that the three-step microcycle method is most effective and is now widely used by many coaches and athletes. In this method, coaches are increasing the load for three microcycles and then unloading for one microcycle to allow the body to regenerate.

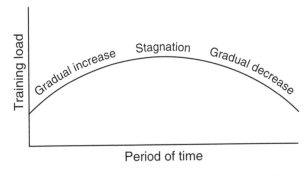

Figure 7.7 Progression of the continuous and gradual loading method of training.

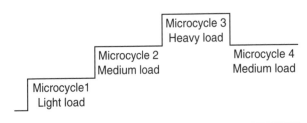

Figure 7.8 The microcycle step method of increasing and unloading training loads.

A study of former Soviet athletes suggested that the volume of training must increase not only from cycle to cycle but from year to year. The study concluded that the volume and intensity should be increased 20% to 40% each year and that time would become a major factor in dealing with the increase in volume (Bompa, 1990).

For today's pole vaulters, who are competing into their mid-30s, the question is how to meet this increase in volume so that stagnation in performance doesn't occur. The trend is to set up workouts that may include double sessions several days per week.

Principle 6: Variety

According to Krzesinski (1993), high-level competition and intense technical work stress the central nervous system and reduce performance, making it necessary at times for a vaulter to take time off to "recharge the battery."

Because the pole vault is so specialized and requires so much intensity just to jump, the coach must develop a variety of drills that simulate the vault. Gymnastic exercises on the high bar, the rope vault, underwater vaulting, and the trampoline are all exercises that simulate some phase of the vault as well as develop coordination, orientation, and technique.

The speed, power, and frequency of the nerve impulses depend on the state of the central nervous system. The force of the muscle contraction and the number of motor units recruited depend on the impulses sent by the central nervous system. Thus, activities designed to reduce the demand on the central nervous system are very important and must be incorporated into the microcycle.

Principle 7: A Technical and Training Model

The coach and athlete must have a technical model that can be studied and based on which they can develop a style of technique and method of training. The style used to carry the pole, the method of lowering the pole, the plant mechanics, the swing, the takeoff, and the turn and extension must be reflected in all drills performed in the daily workouts. The goal is for the athlete to develop a style similar to the model being used.

Pole Vault Training Program

Several concepts must be considered when setting up a vaulting program. Vaulters do not have to be farmed out to camps and left to themselves. Any school can have a successful program by having the vaulters be part of regular team practices. Vaulters do not have to work out by themselves. They can work with sprinters when working on speed; with hurdlers, long jumpers, and triple jumpers when working on power; and with throwers when working on strength. Too often vaulters are left to themselves because the coach fails to assign them to a meaningful workout group. Coaches should decide which components they want the vaulter to work on, then incorporate the vaulter into the group doing that activity. Working with and being part of a group adds fun, challenge, and longevity to the overall athletic experience.

The coach must evaluate the vaulter's strengths and weaknesses and set up workouts based on the results. Each workout must reflect a specific goal the vaulter is working on. Several vaulters working together and pushing each other is the most effective way to produce good vaulters. Coaches and vaulters cannot adopt the American "fast food" philosophy. In today's fast-paced society, we have come to expect immediate results in many facets of our lives, but it is a mistake to apply this philosophy to the vault because the components necessary for success in this event take time to develop. Both coach and vaulter must be patient. Training must be built on a solid foundation consisting of all the components of the vault. Balance is the key to a successful training program. Every component of the vault is linked together (see Figure 7.9). A weak component is like a weak link in a chain and can greatly reduce the effectiveness of all other components.

In developing the pole vault program, the coach and athlete must decide how many times during the year the athlete wants to peak. If the

Figure 7.9 Andrzej Krzesinski's chain concept.

Note. Used with permission of Andrzej Krzesinski.

athlete wants to peak for both the indoor and outdoor championships, the training program should be divided into two plans. If the athlete only wants to peak for the outdoor championships, a single plan can be used. In contrast to the other events presented in this book, the full training year for the pole vault follows.

Period	Phase
Preparation	1. General conditioning
	2. Specific preparation
Competition	3. Early season
	4. Midseason
	5. Unloading
	6. Special preparation
	7. Championships
	8. Peak maintenance
Transition	9. Active recovery from season

In planning workouts, the coach must start with the important competitions at the end of the season and work backward, developing a plan in which the volume of the workload is reduced as the athlete progresses through specific phases and the intensity is gradually increased to bring the athlete to maximum performance for championship competition.

Figure 7.10 shows the relationship between volume and intensity in the annual training plan. The volume and intensity of each exercise must be considered carefully as the program is put together, and coaches must be careful to lay a good foundation of general conditioning before the athlete starts the specific preparation phase.

Workout samples for the pole vault are shown in Figures 7.11 to 7.14. In keeping

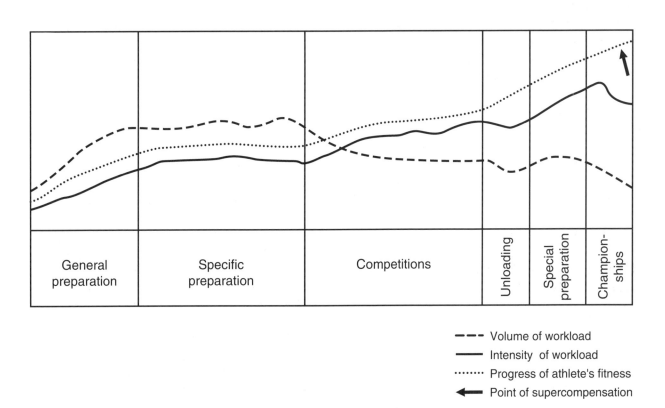

Figure 7.10 Pole vaulter's annual training plan.

General Conditioning Workout

Monday (L)

1. PV drills – vaulter-pole system
2. Weights

Tuesday (M)

1. Gymnastics
2. Sprint power chain 3 × 15
3. Tendon strength – 500

Wednesday (H)

A.M.   PV drills
P.M.   1. Ankle drills
       2. Sprint drills
       3. 2 × 3 × 110 m Recovery:
          Walk back/8 min

Thursday (L)

1. Weights
2. Run/walk – 5 sets

Friday (M)

A.M.   PV drills – vaulter-pole system
P.M.   1. Ankle drills
       2. PV drills
       3. Tendon strength – 500

Saturday (H)

1. Ankle drills
2. Sprint drills
3. Sprint power chain 3 × 15
4. 2 × 4 × 100 m Recovery: 30s/8 min
5. Rope takeoffs

Sunday (L)

Active rest
1. Jog
2. Stretch

Monday (L)

1. PV drills
2. Weights

Tuesday (M)

1. Gymnastics
2. Ankle drills
3. Sprint power chain 3 × 15
4. 2 × 4 × 50 m pulling sled – technique

Wednesday (H)

A.M.   PV drills
P.M.   1. Sprint drills
       2. Tendon strength – 500
       3. Weights

(continued)

Figure 7.11   Sample pole vault workout during the general conditioning phase.

PV drills – vaulter-pole system

1. Setting up first steps
2. Drop to left support
3. L-RT roll both hands
4. RT to takeoff; full extension of arms
5. 8 stride mechanics
   a) Pole at correct angle
   b) Film key positions

Key

RTO	—	Right stride to takeoff stride
RT	—	Right
L	—	Left
TNQ	—	Technique
Fast TNQ	—	Fast, but controlled, concentration on technique
RX	—	Relaxed
H	—	Hurdles
HWT	—	Heavy weight
LT	—	Light
MXV	—	Maximum velocity

Figure 7.11   *(continued)*

Specific Preparation Workout

Thursday (L)

1. Ankle drills
2. Sprint drills
3. 2 × 5 × 50 m, fast TNQ, RX,
   Recovery: 60 s/5 min
4. Sprint power train 4 × 12

Friday (M)

1. Ankle drills
2. Sprint drills
3. Vaulter-pole system drills
4. 14 vaults

Saturday (H)

1. Tendon strength #240
2. Ankle drills
3. Sprint drills
4. 2 × 3 × 150 m Recovery: Walk back, 10 min
   Target: 19.5
5. Weights

Sunday (R)

Rest

Monday (M)

1. Ankle drills
2. Sprint drills
3. Vaulter-pole system
4. 14 vaults
5. Weights

Tuesday (L)

1. Ankle drills
2. Sprint drills
3. 2 × 5 × 60 m sled Recovery: Walk back,
   5 min
4. Sprint power chain 4 × 12

Wednesday (H)

A.M. 1. Gymnastics
      2. Pole drop to left support
      3. Pole drop and plant mechanics to
         right support, RT-L-RT
P.M. 1. Tendon strength #240
      2. Ankle drills
      3. Sprint drills
      4. Vaulter-pole system drills
      5. 14 vaults

Thursday (L)

1. Ankle drills
2. Sprint drills
3. Weights

(continued)

Figure 7.12   Sample pole vault workout during the specific preparation phase.

Friday (M)

1. Ankle drills
2. Sprint drills
3. Vaulter-pole system drills
4. 14 vaults
5. Sprint power chain 4 × 12

Saturday (H)

1. Tendon strength #240
2. Ankle drills
3. Sprint drills
4. Contrast training
   1 × 60 m sled Recovery: 3-5 min; 1 × 60 m
   fast TNQ, RX; 1 × 80 m sled; 1 × 80 m fast
   TNQ, RX; Rest 8 min; 1 × 110 m
5. Weights

PV drills – vaulter-pole system

1. Setting up first steps
2. Drop to left support, wrist above elbow
3. L-RT roll both
4. Pole drop and plant mechanics to right
   support (step before takeoff) RT-L-RT;
   check left elbow, angle of left forearm,
   position of right hand
5. RTO full extension
6. 10-12-14 stride mechanics into box
   a) Pole at correct angle
   b) Film key positions
7. Full approach (using drop diamonds) on
   track*

*Move to 16-plus strides only after mastering #6.

Key

RTO	—	Right stride to takeoff stride
RT	—	Right
L	—	Left
TNQ	—	Technique
Fast TNQ	—	Fast, but controlled, concentration on technique
RX	—	Relaxed
H	—	Hurdles
HWT	—	Heavy weight
LT	—	Light
MXV	—	Maximum velocity

Figure 7.12   *(continued)*

Early Indoor Competition Workout

Monday (H)

A.M.
1. Vaulter-pole system drills
2. Pole drop to left support
3. L-RT stride; roll both hands
4. RT to RT
5. RTO full extension

P.M.
1. Ankle drills
2. Sprint drills
3. Vaulter-pole system
   a) Setting up first steps
   b) Drop to left support
   c) L-RT roll both
   d) RT to RT (check) angle of left forearm
   e) RTO full extension
   f) Plant box
4. 12-14 vaults
5. Sprint power chain

Tuesday (M)

1. Tendon strength
2. Ankle drills
3. Sprint drills
4. 2 × in and outs, Recovery: 5 min
5. Weights

Wednesday (H)

A.M.
1. Vaulter-pole system drills
2. Sprint power chain 3 × 10

P.M.
1. Ankle drills
2. Sprint drills
3. Vaulter-pole system drills
4. 12-14 vaults

Thursday (M)

1. Ankle drills
2. Sprint drills
3. 2 × 5 sled; Walk back/5 min between sets
4. Weights

Friday (L)

At arena
1. Ankle drills
2. Sprint drills
3. Vaulter-pole system drills
4. Takeoffs

Saturday

Competition

Sunday (R)

Rest

(continued)

Figure 7.13 Sample pole vault workout during the early indoor competition phase.

Monday (M)

A.M.
1. Vaulter-pole system drills
   a) Pole drop to L support
   b) Roll both hands
   c) RT to RT
   d) RTO full extension

P.M.
1. Tendon strength
2. Ankle drills
3. Sprint drills
4. Vaulter-pole system drills
5. 12-14 vaults
6. Weights

Tuesday (H)

A.M.
1. Gymnastics
2. Sprint power chain

P.M.
1. Ankle drills
2. Sprint drills
3. Contrast training
   1 × 60 m sled, Recovery: 5 min
   1 × 60 m fast TNQ, RX, Recovery: 5 min
   1 × 80 m sled, Recovery: 5 min
   1 × 80 m fast TNQ, RX
   5 × 55 m H
4. Vaulter-pole system drills

Wednesday (M)

1. Tendon strength
2. Ankle drills
3. Sprint drills
4. Vaulter-pole system drills
5. Weights

Key

RTO	—	Right stride to takeoff stride
RT	—	Right
L	—	Left
TNQ	—	Technique
Fast TNQ	—	Fast, but controlled, concentration on technique
RX	—	Relaxed
H	—	Hurdles
HWT	—	Heavy weight
LT	—	Light
MXV	—	Maximum velocity

Figure 7.13   *(continued)*

Early Outdoor Competition Workout

Thursday (L)

1. Jog, stretch
2. Ankle drills
3. Sprint drills
4. Gymnastics

Friday (M)

A.M.
1. Tendon strength
2. Vaulter-pole system drills
P.M.
1. Ankle drills
2. Sprint drills
3. Vault

Saturday (R)

Travel day

Sunday (C)

Relays

Monday (L)

1. Tendon strength
2. Ankle drills
3. Sprint drills
4. Sprint power chain

Tuesday (H)

A.M.
1. Vaulter-pole system drills
2. Gymnastics
P.M.
1. Light tendon strength
2. Ankle drills
3. Sprint drills
4. Sprint preparation
   a) 3 × 90, 30/75, 30/85, 30/95
   b) 3 × 30 MXV
5. Speed development
   One set of contrasts
   1) 1 × 80 m chute
   2) 1 × 30 m MXV
   3) 1 × 30 m HWT sled
   4) 1 × 30 m MXV
   5) 1 × 40 m double sled
   6) 1 × 30 m MXV
   7) 1 × 60 m LT sled
   8) 3 × 55 H (24"–8.70 cm)

Wednesday (M)

1. Tendon strength
2. Ankle drills
3. Sprint drills
4. Weights

Thursday (M)

1. Ankle drills
2. Sprint drills
3. Vaulter-pole system drills
4. Vault

(continued)

Figure 7.14   Sample pole vault workout during the early outdoor competition phase.

Friday (H)

A.M.
1. Tendon strength
2. Gymnastics

P.M.
1. Ankle drills
2. Sprint drills
3. Sprint prep
   a) 3 × 90 m 30/75 30/85 30/95
   b) 3 × 30 m MXV
4. Speed development
   One set of contrasts
   1) 1 × 30 m HWT sled
   2) 1 × 55 H
   3) 1 × 40 m double sled
   4) 2 × 30 m MXV
   5) 1 × 60 m LT sled
   6) 1 × 55 m H
   7) Rest 8–12 min
   8) 1 × 60 m MXV

Saturday (L)

1. Tendon strength
2. Weights

Key

RTO	—	Right stride to takeoff stride
RT	—	Right
L	—	Left
TNQ	—	Technique
Fast TNQ	—	Fast, but controlled, concentration on technique
RX	—	Relaxed
H	—	Hurdles
HWT	—	Heavy weight
LT	—	Light
MXV	—	Maximum velocity

Figure 7.14   *(continued)*

with the training year outlined above, workouts are presented for the general conditioning phase (Figure 7.11), the specific preparation phase (Figure 7.12), early indoor competition (Figure 7.13), and early outdoor competition (Figure 7.14).

Summary

Setting up an annual program for high school or college athletes can be difficult. In many high school districts the season is limited to 3 to 4 months, with competitions being held twice a week throughout the season.

It is easier to plan a college program, but still problematic. College athletes need to make qualifying marks to reach the national championships. The training cycle is constantly interrupted because early meets are often held on good facilities, and the athletes need to take advantage of the good facilities to reach qualifying marks. Both coaches and athletes realize that these interruptions are not ideal, but because the athlete needs the best chance to qualify, coaches modify the training cycle.

The elite athlete, though appearing to have the best chance to follow a strict training system, also encounters many obstacles. In the last decade the availability of prize money has made elite vaulters make sudden changes in their training programs because of the chance to compete in early meets and earn money, money that can buy the time to train and stay in the sport longer. Another problem for the elite American vaulter is balancing competition and training throughout the indoor and early outdoor seasons in the U.S. and the following longer European season. In addition, in many cases the elite vaulter's schedule in Europe depends on how well he performs from week to week, so the vaulter faces difficult questions: How many times can I interrupt my training? How many competitions should I have? How can I compete without getting physically and emotionally drained, and still make money? But it is very important to remember that elite vaulters must continue to increase annual training volume, or stagnation will occur.

As you can see, each level has its own set of problems. Careful planning is necessary if the athlete is to reach his or her maximum potential as a vaulter.

Bibliography

Adamczewski, H. (1991). *Line Drawing of Female Vaulter*. Leipzig, Germany.

Bompa, T. O. (1990). *Theory and methodology of training*. Dubuque, IA: Kendall/Hunt.

Bullard, E., & Knuth, L. (1977). *Triple jump encyclopedia*. Pasadena, CA: Athletic Press.

Dapena, J., Feltner, M., & Bahomonde, R. (1986, December). *Men's high jump #5* (USOC/TAC Scientific Services Program).

Dapena, J., Paklin, I., & Conway, H. (1987, October). *Men's high jump #7* (USOC/TAC Scientific Services Program).

Dapena, J., & Vaughn, R. (1993). *Men's high jump #10*.

Doolittle, D. (1988). *TAC level II coaches manual*. Indianapolis: USA Track and Field.

Dyson, G. (1977). *Mechanics of athletics*. New York: Holmes and Meier.

Feroah, T. (1992). Approach velocities of high school vaulters at the USA Track and Field Pole Vault Summit. Reno Orthopedic Clinic, Center for Biomechanical Research, Sparks, Nevada.

Gros, H., & Kunkel, V. (1987). Biomechanical analysis of the pole vault. *International Amateur Athletic Federation Scientific Report on the II World Championships in Athletics, Rome 1987*. Monaco: International Amateur Athletic Federation.

Hay, J. (1973). *The biomechanics of sports techniques of athletics (2nd ed.)*. Englewood Cliffs, NJ: Prentice-Hall.

Hay, J. (1983a). *The biomechanics of the long jump* (USOC/TAC Scientific Services Program).

Hay, J. (1983b). *Exercise and physical education*.

Hay, J. (1984). Comparative data of velocities and angles of takeoff in the long jump. Sports Sciences.

Hay, J. (1987). [Analysis of Willie Banks] (USOC/TAC Scientific Services Program).

Hay, J. (1988). [Analysis of Kenny Harrison] (USOC/TAC Scientific Services Program).

Hay, J. (1990). [Analysis of Sheila Hudson.]

Hay, J. (1990, June). The biomechanics of triple jump techniques. In G.-P. Bruggeman & J.K. Ruhl (Eds.), *Techniques in Athletics: Conference Proceedings*. Cologne: Sport und Buch Strauss.

Hay, J. (1991). [Analysis of Mike Powell.]

Hay, J., & Feuerbach, J.W. (1989). *Biomechanical analysis of technique of Carl Lewis competing in the long jump at selected meets, 1982-1987*. Iowa City, IA: University of Iowa. (TAC/USOC Scientific Services Program)

Hay, J., Bing, Y., & Hayes, D. (1990). *Triple jump* (TAC/USOC Scientific Services Program).

Jacoby, E. (1983). *Applied techniques in track and field*. Champaign, IL: Leisure Press.

Jacoby, E. (1993). [General analysis of flop high jump]. Unpublished paper.

Kenn, J. (1994). *Strength training procedures—lecture and lab manual*. Unpublished master's thesis, Boise State University, Boise, ID.

Krzesinski, A. (1993, July). *Annual Training Programs*. Paper presented at USA Track and Field Pole Vault Clinic in Fresno, California.

Krzesinski, A. (1994, May). *Pole vault safety*. Paper presented at USA Track and Field West Region pole vault development meeting in San Jose, California.

McGinnis, P. (1991a). Approach Velocities of Elite Vaulters at Major Competitions.

McGinnis, P. (1991b). Pole Vault Sequences.

Petrov, V. (1994). [USA Track and Field Pole Vault Summit, Reno.]

Popplewell, G. (1978). *Modern weight lifting and power lifting*. London: Faber and Faber.

Ritzdorf, W., & Conrad, A. (1987). Biomechanical analysis of the high jump. *International Amateur Athletic Federation Scientific Report on the II World Championships in Athletics, Rome 1987*. Monaco: International Amateur Athletic Federation.

Sasaki, H., Kobayashi, K., & Ae, M. (Eds.). (1994). *Techniques of the world-class track and field athletes*. Tokyo: Baseball Magazine Publishing Company, Ltd.

Schmolinsky, G. (1978). *Track and Field*. Berlin: Sport Verlag.

Susanka, P., Jurdik, M., Koukal, J., Kratky, P., & Velebil, V. (1987). Biomechanical analysis of the triple jump. *International Amateur Athletic Federation Scientific Report on the II World Championships in Athletics, Rome 1987*. Monaco: International Amateur Athletic Federation.

Tidow, G. (1989). Model technique analysis sheet for the horizontal jumps. Part I: The long jump. *IAAF Quarterly Magazine for Technical Research*, **4**, 53-62.

Verhoshansky, Y. (1967). *Depth jumping in the training of jumpers*. Legkaya Atletika, USSR.

Index

About the Authors

Ed Jacoby has been coaching track and field since 1961. During that time, he has worked with athletes at virtually every level, including high school, junior college, and NCAA Divisions I and II. He served as assistant coach at the 1992 Olympic Games in Barcelona and as head coach for the 1993 World Championship team. Over the years, he has coached 4 national champions, 26 All-Americans, and 4 Olympians.

Jacoby has held various positions within USA Track & Field, including men's development chair, men's high jump coordinator, and Level I and II instructor. He has been head track and field coach at Boise State University since 1973.

Ed Jacoby

Bob Fraley and his son, Doug, collaborated on the pole vault chapter of this book. Bob has been coaching pole vaulters since 1959. He is the chairman of USA Track & Field Pole Vault Development and the sprints and jump coach at Fresno State University. Doug is a 3-time NCAA-champion pole vaulter who has competed in the European Grand Prix Circuit since 1986.

Bob Fraley

More great track and field resources

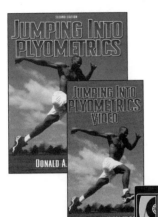

Jumping Into Plyometrics

(Second Edition)

Donald A. Chu, PhD

1998 • Paperback • 184 pp • Item PCHU0846
ISBN 0-88011-846-6 • $15.95 ($23.95 Canadian)

Jumping Into Plyometrics Video

(35-minute videotape)

1993 • 1/2" VHS • Item MCHU0246
ISBN 0-87322-509-0 • $29.95 ($44.95 Canadian)

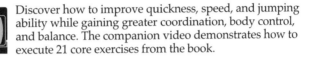
Discover how to improve quickness, speed, and jumping
ability while gaining greater coordination, body control,
and balance. The companion video demonstrates how to
execute 21 core exercises from the book.

High-Performance Training for Track and Field

(Second Edition)

William J. Bowerman and William H. Freeman

1991 • Paperback • 264 pp • Item PBOW0390
ISBN 0-88011-390-1 • $24.00 ($35.95 Canadian)

Discusses training theories and how to apply them to training
programs. Includes workouts that can be adapted for any athlete,
regardless of age, sex, or stage of athletic development.

The Athletics Congress's Track and Field Coaching Manual

(Second Edition)

**The Athletics Congress's Development Committees
with Vern Gambetta, Editor**

1989 • Paperback • 240 pp • Item PTAC0332
ISBN 0-88011-332-4 • $22.00 ($32.95 Canadian)

Use this handbook to enhance your athletes' knowledge of proper
form and mechanics. Also includes complete instructions for
planning training sessions and hosting competitions.

Fundamentals of Track and Field

(Second Edition)

Gerry A. Carr

1999 • Paperback • Approx 272 pp • Item PCAR0008
ISBN 0-7360-0008-9 • $19.95 ($29.95 Canadian)

All the information you need for teaching track and field skills to
beginners. Contains more than 300 illustrations of techniques and
teaching progressions.

Prices subject to change.

To place an order: U.S. customers call **TOLL-FREE 1-800-747-4457**;
customers outside of U.S. use the appropriate telephone number/address shown in the front of this book.

HUMAN KINETICS
The Premier Publisher for Sports & Fitness
www.humankinetics.com

2335